INTRODUCTION TO
Computer Simulations for
Integrated STEM
College Education

INTRODUCTION TO
Computer Simulations for Integrated STEM College Education

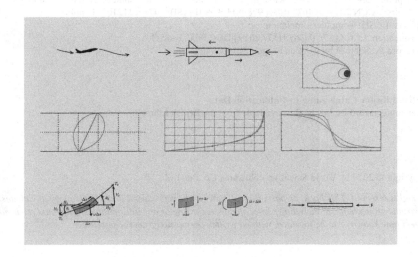

Mohamed M Hafez
William E Tavernetti

University of California, Davis, USA

 **World Scientific**

NEW JERSEY · LONDON · SINGAPORE · BEIJING · SHANGHAI · HONG KONG · TAIPEI · CHENNAI · TOKYO

Published by

World Scientific Publishing Co. Pte. Ltd.

5 Toh Tuck Link, Singapore 596224

USA office: 27 Warren Street, Suite 401-402, Hackensack, NJ 07601

UK office: 57 Shelton Street, Covent Garden, London WC2H 9HE

Library of Congress Cataloging-in-Publication Data

Names: Hafez, M. M., author. | Tavernetti, William Edward, author.

Title: Introduction to computer simulations for integrated STEM college education /
    Mohamed M. Hafez, William E. Tavernetti, University of California, Davis, USA.

Description: New Jersey : World Scientific, [2019] | Includes bibliographical references and index.

Identifiers: LCCN 2019039407 | ISBN 9789811209901 | ISBN 9789811210761 (pbk)

Subjects: LCSH: Computer simulation.

Classification: LCC QA76.9.C65 H337 2019 | DDC 003/.3--dc23

LC record available at https://lccn.loc.gov/2019039407

British Library Cataloguing-in-Publication Data

A catalogue record for this book is available from the British Library.

For any available supplementary material, please visit
https://www.worldscientific.com/worldscibooks/10.1142/11542#t=suppl

Printed in Singapore

Preface

Computers have become an essential tool for students and professionals across all disciplines and especially in modern science applications. Today, physical phenomena, engineering projects and processes can be readily simulated based on mathematical modeling. Computers are used in a wide range of technologies, from astronautics to robotics. To introduce college students (freshmen to senior students) to this field of simulations, simple algorithms which are easy to program and can be applied to a range of problems of interest in their curriculum are required. The purpose of this book is to meet this need in a friendly and informal manner. The prerequisites are a first course in calculus and a first course in computer programming (Matlab is used to produce all the results discussed in the book). Matlab is preferred for students, but GNU Octave (open source Matlab) can also be downloaded and used for free. Excel, or a spreadsheet program, can also be used for most of the problems in this text.

The book consists of three parts. In the first part, numerical solution of algebraic equations, numerical approximations of integrals and derivatives as well as introductions to simple ordinary differential equations describing elementary functions are presented. In the section for modules, numerical solutions of ordinary differential equations, first and second order, initial and boundary value problems are presented using simple algorithms. More general linear differential equations with constant and variable coefficients are solved with the same algorithms, as well as important nonlinear differential equations. In the next section, several examples are given placing emphasis on dealing with nonlinearity where computers are indispensable for obtaining the solutions. The second part deals with applications in dynamics and electrical circuits, structural mechanics, fluid mechanics as well as heat transfer, chemical reaction and combustion problems. The focus in this section is on the numerical solution to these problems. In the third part, biographies of famous mathematicians and scientists, whose works are relevant to the material in the book, are briefly presented.

The book can be used by college students who are interested in computer simulations of STEM problems. The main feature of the book is its simple approach to solve several numerical problems on the computer and the large number of applications in different areas using the same simple algorithms. The book is not a substitute for other books introducing the physics, chemistry and programming, for example, but it will set a foundation for future learning in more advanced studies that involve numerical simulations and help students develop confidence in this material. Indeed, there are many good books teaching Matlab programming. There are also many excellent books on numerical analysis with proofs of theorems, or on sophisticated numerical methods for applications in specialized areas, but in this book emphasis is placed on the common thread among certain problems solved by the simple methods presented in the modules. The present integrated approach makes it easy to understand the applications of numerical methods to many physical problems and the students will see the similarity of the treatment of these problems. Thus, the book can serve as a companion to texts on differential equations, numerical methods, as well as science and engineering courses. It is a source of projects for teachers, and for students as a self-study, where they can solve the problems on their own and compare their results with the solutions provided by the authors.

I. MATH

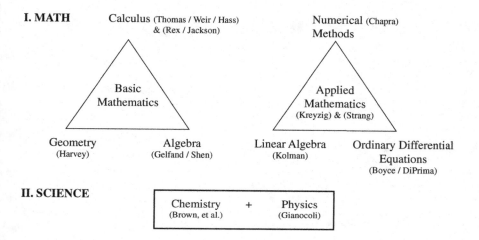

II. SCIENCE

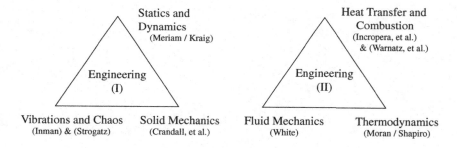

III. ENGINEERING

Roadmap for Integrated Stem Education
(with suggested references)

Contents

Preface   v

1   Introduction   1

  1.1   Discussion of the Book Contents   2

Part I   Mathematical and Numerical Methods

2   Basic Mathematics Prerequisites   11

  2.1   Geometry   11

  2.2   Algebra   11

  2.3   Calculus   12

3   Applied Mathematics   14

  3.1   Numerical Solutions of Algebraic Equations   14

    3.1.1   Systems of Linear Algebraic Equations   14

    3.1.2   Nonlinear Problems   18

    3.1.3   Kepler's Equation for Planetary Orbits   20

    3.1.4   Root Finding and Newton Fractals   20

    3.1.5   Global Positioning System   24

  3.2   Numerical Methods for Approximations of Integrals

       and Derivatives   25

    3.2.1   Approximations of Integrals and Derivatives   25

    3.2.2   Accuracy of the Approximations for Derivatives

          (Forward, Backward and Center Differences)   . . .   28

  3.3   Introduction to Ordinary Differential Equations   . . .   29

    3.3.1   Differential Equations Representing Polynomial

          Functions   29

    3.3.2   Differential Equations Representing Exponential,

          Trigonometric, and Hyperbolic Functions   31

    3.3.3   Summary of Differential Equations   34

4   Numerical Modules   35

  4.1   Introduction to Numerical Solution of Ordinary

       Differential Equations   35

4.2   Module 1: Scalar First-Order Differential
       Equation   39
       4.2.1   System of First-Order Equations   41
4.3   Module 2: Second-Order Differential Equations
       (Initial Value Problems)   42
4.4   Module 3: Second-Order Differential Equations
       (Boundary Value Problems)   43
4.5   Module 4: Eigenvalue Problems (Characteristic Value
       Problems)   45
4.6   Numerical Stability   47
       4.6.1   Numerical Stability: First-Order Equations   47
       4.6.2   Numerical Stability: Second-Order Differential
                Equations   50

5   **Numerical Solution of Differential Equations**   **52**

5.1   Linear Differential Equations with Constant
       Coefficients   52
       5.1.1   Mass-Spring System   52
       5.1.2   Stability Analysis for Mass-Spring System   54
       5.1.3   Scalar Non-Homogeneous Damped Mass Spring
                System   55
       5.1.4   Pure Resonance   56
       5.1.5   Beating Phenomena   57
       5.1.6   Electric Circuits and Analog Computers   58
       5.1.7   Coupled Masses System: Free Vibration   60
       5.1.8   Coupled Damping System: Brouwer's
                Gyroscopic Effect   62
       5.1.9   Coupled Stiffness System: Landing Gears   65
       5.1.10   Boundary Value Problem for Second-Order
                Differential Equation with Constant
                Coefficients   66
       5.1.11   Second-Order Equation with Small Parameter . . .   68
5.2   Linear Differential Equations with Variable
       Coefficients   69
       5.2.1   Example of First-Order Differential Equation . . .   69
       5.2.2   Bessel Functions of the First Kind   71
       5.2.3   Airy Functions   71
       5.2.4   Mathieu Equation   72
       5.2.5   Euler–Cauchy Equation   73

    5.2.6   Legendre Polynomials 77
    5.2.7   Boundary Layer with Linear Differential
            Equation 78
  5.3   Nonlinear Differential Equations 78
    5.3.1   Finite Time Blow-up 78
    5.3.2   Spontaneous Singularities 81
    5.3.3   Bernoulli Equation 82
    5.3.4   Saddle Node Bifurcations 84
    5.3.5   Transcritical Bifurcations 85
    5.3.6   Pitchfork Bifurcations 86
    5.3.7   Hopf Bifucations 87
    5.3.8   Jerk Equation and Its Chaotic Solution 88
    5.3.9   Lorenz Equation and Its Chaotic Solution 89
    5.3.10 Nonlinear Spring: Pendulums and the Phase
            Plane 92
    5.3.11 Nonlinear Spring: Duffing Oscillator 95
    5.3.12 Nonlinear Damping: Van der Pol Oscillator 96
    5.3.13 Nonlinear Damping: Rayleigh Equation 96
    5.3.14 Rayleigh Equation as a Singular Perturbation
            Problem 100
    5.3.15 Nonlinear Mass: Relativistic Restoring Force 101
    5.3.16 Nonlinear Boundary Value Problems 102

Part II   Applications in Science and Engineering

6   Dynamics and Vibrations   107

  6.1   Rocket Dynamics in Space
        (Tsiolkovsky Equation) 107
  6.2   Vertical Motion of Launch Vehicle 109
  6.3   Parachute Equation with Constant Drag
        Coefficient 110
  6.4   Projectiles and Orbital Mechanics
        of Two-Body Problem 110
    6.4.1   Cannon Fire Over a Flat Surface 110
    6.4.2   Cannon Fire with Linear Drag 112
    6.4.3   Two Body Problem: Earth
            and a Satellite 113
  6.5   Stability of Orbits 115
  6.6   Phugoid Motion and Pendulum 116
  6.7   Why Airplanes Have Tails? 119

7   Solid and Structural Mechanics   120

   7.1   Tension in Cable 120
   7.2   Bending of Beams 122
   7.3   Torsion of Shafts 123
   7.4   Buckling of Columns 124

8   Fluid Mechanics   126

   8.1   Viscous Flow: Viscous Flows in Channel 126
   8.2   Viscous Flow: Boundary Layer Over Flat Plate
        with Suction 128
   8.3   Laval Nozzle: Quasi-One-Dimensional Flow 128
   8.4   Shock Viscous Layer 131

9   Heat Transfer   132

   9.1   Heat Transfer: Newton's Law of Cooling 133
   9.2   Heat Transfer: Stefan-Boltzmann Law
        of Radiation 133
   9.3   Heat Transfer: Convection and Radiation 134
   9.4   Heat Transfer: Heat Conduction with Heat Source . . 134
   9.5   Heat Transfer: Heat Conduction Through
        Thin Fin 135
   9.6   Heat Transfer: Ablation 137

10   Chemical Reactions   138

   10.1   Chemical Reactions: One-Step Irreversible
        Reaction $A \to B$ 138
   10.2   Chemical Reactions: Several Species 139
   10.3   Chemical Oscillations: Belousov–Zhabotinsky
        Equations 140
   10.4   Chemical Chaos: Rossler Equations 141

11   Combustion   143

   11.1   Combustion: Thermal Explosion Theory 143
   11.2   Combustion: Ignition Based on
        Newton's Cooling Law 143
   11.3   Combustion: Ignition Based on
        Fourier's Conduction Law 145
   11.4   Combustion: Solid Propellant Burning 146

Part III Historical Biographies

12 Greek Mathematicians   **149**

12.1 Pythagoras of Samos (about 570–495 BCE) 149
12.2 Euclid of Alexandria (about 365–275 BCE) 150
12.3 Apollonius of Perga (about 262–190 BCE) 152
12.4 Archimedes of Syracuse (287–212 BCE) 153
12.5 Hero of Alexandria (about 10–70 CE) 155

13 Pioneers in Mathematics   **156**

13.1 René Descartes (1596–1650) 157
13.2 Christian Huygens (1629–1695) 158
13.3 Isaac Newton (1643–1727) 158
13.4 Gottfried Wilhelm Leibniz (1646–1716) 160
13.5 Leonhard Euler (1707–1783) 161
13.6 Daniel Bernoulli (1700–1782) 163
13.7 Carl Friedrich Gauss (1777–1855) 164
13.8 Georg Friedrich Bernhard Riemann (1826–1866) . . . 165

14 French School of Mathematics   **166**

14.1 Pierre de Fermat (1601–1665) 166
14.2 Blaise Pascal (1623–1662) 167
14.3 Pierre-Simon, marquis de Laplace (1749–1827) 168
14.4 Augustin Louis Cauchy (1789–1857) 169
14.5 Jean-Baptiste Joseph Fourier (1768–1830) 170
14.6 Jean le Rond d'Alembert (1717–1783) 171
14.7 Siméon Denis Poisson (1781–1840) 171
14.8 Joseph-Louis Lagrange (1736–1813) 172
14.9 Jules Henri Poincaré (1854–1912) 173

15 British School of Mathematics   **173**

15.1 Brook Taylor (1685–1731) 174
15.2 William Rowan Hamilton (1805–1865) 174
15.3 Sir George Stokes (1819–1903) 175

16 Pioneers in Science and Engineering   **175**

16.1 Leonardo da Vinci (1452–1519) 176
16.2 Nicolaus Copernicus (1473–1543) 177

16.3 Galileo Galilei (1564–1642) 178
16.4 Johannes Kepler (1571–1630) 179
16.5 Konstantin Eduardovich Tsiolkovsky
      (1857–1935) 180

17 Structures and Vibrations   181

17.1 Robert Hooke (1635–1703) 181
17.2 John William Strutt, 3rd Baron Rayleigh
      (1842–1919) 183

18 Fluid and Aerodynamics   184

18.1 Heinrich Gustav Magnus (1802–1870) 184
18.2 Nikolay Yegorovich Zhukovsky (1847–1921) 184
18.3 Ludwig Prandtl (1875–1953) 185
18.4 Ernst Mach (1838–1916) 186
18.5 Osborne Reynolds (1842–1912) 187
18.6 Claude Louis Marie Henri Navier (1785–1836) 188
18.7 Gustaf de Laval (1845–1913) 188

19 Thermodynamics and Heat Transfer   189

19.1 James Prescott Joule (1818–1889) 190
19.2 Hermann Ludwig Ferdinand von Helmholtz
      (1821–1894) 191
19.3 Nicolas Léonard Sadi Carnot (1796–1832) 192
19.4 Rudolf Clausius (1822–1888) 193
19.5 William Thomson, 1st Baron Kelvin
      (1824–1907) 193
19.6 Ludwig Eduard Boltzmann (1844–1906) 194
19.7 Josiah Willard Gibbs (1839–1903) 195

20 Chemistry and Combustion   195

20.1 Antoine-Laurent de Lavoisier (1743–1794) 196
20.2 Svante Arrhenius (1859–1927) 197

21 Electricity and Magnetism   198

21.1 Charles-Augustin de Coulomb (1736–1806) 198
21.2 Gustav Robert Kirchhoff (1824–1887) 199
21.3 James Clerk Maxwell (1831–1879) 199

Part IV Miscellanea

22 Summary, Final Remarks and Takeaways   203

22.1 Basic Mathematics: Geometry, Algebra
and Calculus 203
22.2 Elementary Functions and Their
Differential Equations 205
22.3 Numerical Methods 207
22.4 Numerical Solutions of Differential Equations 209
22.5 Applications in Science and Engineering 210

23 Appendices   211

23.1 Basics of Programming 211
23.2 Thomas Algorithm for Tridiagonal Matrix 211

24 General References   212

24.1 Math 212
24.2 Science and Engineering 213

Index   215

1. Introduction

Recently, there is a great emphasis on STEM education since these fields are important for a majority of jobs in academia and industry. The four components of STEM are mathematics, science, engineering and technology, in this order. Mathematics is based on logic, starting with assumptions, followed by induction and conclusions. It is the language of science, precise and concise. On the other hand, science is the law of nature. Physics and chemistry are necessary to understand biology, geology and cosmology namely life, earth and space sciences. Engineering deals with design, analysis and control of processes and products. For example, mechanical and aerospace engineering deals with cars, airplanes, rockets, and satellites, while civil and environmental engineering deals with structures, buildings, bridges, hydraulics and pollution. Electrical engineering deals with generators, motors, transmission lines and communications, while chemical and materials engineering deals with chemical reactions, combustion as well as properties of materials and their behaviors. This is just a brief synopsis, and there are other types like agricultural, biomedical, petroleum, nuclear, ocean engineering, etc. Finally technology deals with manufacturing processes and practical considerations like machines and factories, efficiency, safety and sustainability. For all of the above, computers play a vital role in many ways.

Computer hardware and software introduced major changes in our civilization. After 50 years, Moore's law is still valid and computers capabilities, memory and speed doubles every other year.[1] Sooner or later this trend will end with another phase of saturation. By that time, other types of computers will emerge, for example optical or quantum computing are very promising. The revolution introduced by computers has just begun and the next generation should enjoy more of it.

---

[1]Golio, Mike. 50 years of Moore's Law. *Proceedings of the IEEE*, Vol. 103, No. 10, October 2015.

1.1   Discussion of the Book Contents

The purpose of this book is to prepare students to use computers in simulations. High school math and science as well as some computer programming are the main prerequisites. Basic mathematics including a working knowledge of geometry, algebra and calculus is the foundation, which will be applied to linear algebra, differential equations and numerical methods. Our approach is to start with the four elementary functions: polynomials, exponential, hyperbolic and trigonometric functions. The definitions and properties of these functions are taught in high school. Students should plot these functions and study carefully their behaviors. It turns out that these functions can be described by relations among their derivatives. For example, consider the polynomial function. The simplest possible function is $u = \text{constant} = 1$. The derivative of a constant is zero, the function does not change, and hence

$$\frac{du}{dt} = 0.$$

Using the fundamental theorem of calculus, we can obtain $u(x)$ by simply integrating both sides of the equation as

$$\int \frac{du}{dt} dt = \int 0 \, dt = 0$$

or, $\int du = 0$, which implies $u + \text{constant} = 0$. The constant of integration can be obtained if we specifiy $u(t)$ at $t = 0$, say $u(0) = 1$, and hence $u(t) = 1$ would then be a solution of the differential equation and the initial condition. The next simplest example is

$$u(t) = t$$

where by differentiation on both sides we obtain the differential equations

$$\frac{du}{dt} = 1$$

subject to one initial condition, typically $u(0) = c$. Using the fundamental theorem of calculus, we can again obtain the solution satisfying the differential equation and the initial condition. Similarly, the exponential function can be uniquely described by the property that at any point the function is equal to its derivative. This differential equation for u as a function of t, over a domain from $t = 0$ to $t = T$, is

$$\frac{du}{dt} = u,$$

can be integrated to produce $u = e^t$, provided the constant of integration is given from an initial condition, say $u(0) = 1$. We can easily verify that the exponential function satisfies the differential equation and the initial condition at t equal zero. Notice here we construct the differential equation to describe a certain function. In other words, we know the solution of the differential equation a priori. As an extension to the above argument, one can consider the problem, where α is a real number,

$$\frac{du}{dt} = \alpha u,$$

together with the initial conditions $u(0) = 1$. The solution of the differential equation is then $u(t) = e^{\alpha t}$. This can be easily shown by defining the new variable $\bar{t} = \alpha t$, hence the differential equation becomes

$$\frac{du}{d\bar{t}} = u,$$

and $u(0) = 1$, hence the solution is $u(\bar{t}) = e^{\bar{t}} = e^{\alpha t}$. For $\alpha = 1$, the solutions grows exponentially, while for $\alpha = -1$ the solution decays exponentially. A combination of e^t and e^{-t} produces hyperbolic functions, for example,

$$\frac{e^t + e^{-t}}{2} = \cosh(t), \qquad \frac{e^t - e^{-t}}{2} = \sinh(t).$$

The differential equations describing these functions is

$$\frac{d^2 u}{dt^2} - u = 0.$$

This can be easily verified since the derivatives of these functions are known from their definitions in terms of the exponential functions. The difference between the two solutions are the constants of integration. Since we have second derivatives, we have to integrate the differential equation twice to obtain $u(t)$. There are two constants of integration, so we need two conditions to determine these two constants. To have $cosh(t)$ as a solution, we can impose, $u(0) = 1$ and $\frac{du}{dt}(0) = 0$, while to have $\sinh(t)$, we impose instead $u(0) = 0$ and $\frac{du}{dt}(0) = 1$. A more general equation is

$$\frac{d^2u}{dt^2} + \alpha u = 0$$

when $\alpha = -1$ we have hyperbolic functions, as above, and when $\alpha = 1$ we have trigonometric functions $\cos(t)$ and $\sin(t)$ which satisfy the equation. Again, there are appropriate initial conditions associated with the trigonometric functions and to have $\cos(t)$ as a solution, we can impose, $u(0) = 1$ and $\frac{du}{dt}(0) = 0$, while to have $\sin(t)$ we impose instead $u(0) = 0$ and $\frac{du}{dt}(0) = 1$. All of these example solutions make use of ideas from integral calculus, where the solutions are known a priori. The idea is that you are solving a problem that essentially you already know the answer to, and now the next idea is to find the solutions using numerical methods without knowing the results from calculus.

To find a numerical solution of the differential equation (with the initial conditions) we use computers and compare the results with the exact solution, which is known from calculus. There are three typical steps of this process.

1. (Grids): The generation of a grid via discretizing the domain by a finite number of grid points or nodes.
2. (Schemes): Replacing the governing equation by algebraic equations at the nodes.
3. (Solvers): Solving the algebraic equations to produce the numerical solutions at the nodes.

To implement these steps, let the domain of interest start from $t = 0$ to $t = T$. Then, take n-elements covering the domain, so that there are $n + 1$ nodes in total. The size of each element, Δt, is given by the relations $n\Delta t = T$, or $\Delta t = T/n$, where $t_{i+1} = t_i + \Delta t$. To discretize the equation, use the finite difference method. An example of a finite difference is to approximate the definition of derivative

$$\frac{du}{dt} = \lim_{\Delta t \to 0} \frac{u(t + \Delta t) - u(t)}{\Delta t} \approx \frac{u_{i+1} - u_i}{\Delta t}.$$

Hence, for example the equation

$$\frac{du}{dt} = \alpha u$$

is replaced by the difference equations

$$\frac{u_{i+1} - u_i}{\Delta t} = \alpha u_n, \quad i = 1, \ldots, n-1.$$

The third step is to use the recursive relation

$$u_{i+1} = u_i + \alpha \Delta t u_n = (1 + \alpha \Delta t) u_i.$$

To calculate the solutions at all the nodes for $i = 2, \ldots, n$ we need the initial condition $u(1) = 1$ at $t = 0$. Alternatively, we can integrate both sides of the equation

$$\int_t^{t+\Delta t} du = \int_t^{t+\Delta t} \alpha u(t) \, dt \Rightarrow u_{i+1} - u_i = \int_t^{t+\Delta t} \alpha u(t) \, dt.$$

We can use the rectangle rule to evaluate the right hand side, namely

$$\int_t^{t+\Delta t} \alpha u(t) \, dt \approx \alpha u_i \cdot \Delta t$$

and hence we obtain the recursive relation

$$u_{i+1} = u_i + \alpha \Delta t \cdot u_i = (1 + \alpha \Delta t) u_i$$

which is the same relation we obtained by approximating the derivative by finite differences. Other possibilities exist, for example we can use the trapezoidal rule as will be discussed later in the text. In general, the numerical approximations of derivatives are constructed using Taylor series expansion indicating the order of error in each case. Also, the numerical stability of the solutions of the difference equations is studied for the simple cases considered.

Once we establish that the numerical solution can be a good approximation to the exact solution, a solution that is known ahead of time for these cases, we can improve the accuracy of the numerical approximation by using more nodes, i.e. smaller step size.

Next, it will be shown that we can solve more general ordinary differential equations with the same strategy. For example, the mass-spring-damping system

$$m\frac{d^2u}{dt^2} + c\frac{du}{dt} + ku = f$$

can be solved numerically using the above three steps, even if m, c, k are functions of time, or the unknown $u(t)$! In general an exact solution is not available to compare with, but techniques can be developed to check the accuracy of the numerical solution. The numerical solutions of differential equations are the main topic in this book and applications in many fields will follow in a straightforward manner that the students will be able to use.

The homogeneous equation represents the transient behavior of the solution, which can be described by exponential functions. Since the derivative of an exponential function is an exponential function, the differential equation is reduced to an algebraic equation with two roots, and the solution is a linear combination of two exponential functions. If the root is repeated, then a special treatment is required.The system is unstable if small disturbances will grow in time. To guarantee bounded solutions, the following conditions must be satisfied: $k > 0$ (static stability) and $c > 0$ (dynamic stability). These conditions mean that the spring has a restoring force and the damping resist the motion, hence it is associated with energy dissipation. The topic of stability is very important and appears in many applications. There is also an analogy between mechanical and electrical circuits governed by the same equation, with inductance, resistance and the inverse of capacitance corresponding to mass, damping and spring stiffness respectively. This analogy is the essence of analog computers.

Several examples of linear differential equations with variable coefficients are considered, representing special functions including Bessel, Airy, Legendre polynomials and Matthieu functions. Numerical solutions reveal the properties of the special functions in a simple way. Important nonlinear differential equations are also considered in details, including nonlinear pendulum, soft and hard Springs of Duffing equation, nonlinear damping of Van der Pol and Rayleigh equations as well as non-linear mass reflecting relativistic correction. Sub and super critical pitchfork bifurcations, limit cycles and Hopf bifurcation, as well as chaos problems, are solved numerically with the same simple algorithms mentioned earlier. Finally, a nonlinear two point boundary value problem is discussed.

In Part II, several applications in science and engineering are addressed using simple examples. In the section on dynamics and vibrations there are several examples such as: launching rockets, the two body problem of orbital mechanics, stability of circular orbits and spin stabilization of satellites, as well as the stability of airplanes in phugoid motion. These problems are all analyzed using numerical solutions of the associated differential equations.

A section of structural mechanics follows, including tension in cables, torsion of shafts, bending of beams and buckling of struts. Buckling of struts is a classical example of the eigenvalue problem, where the load aligned along the axis of the strut is the Eigen (or characteristic) value and the shape of the deflected strut is the Eigen vector (or Eigenfunction in this case). With loads less than the critical value the strut will remain straight, and does not buckle. The section on fluid dynamics includes examples such steady, two dimensional, incompressible, viscous fluid flow between two plates, and boundary layer development over a flat plate with suction. Additionally, the inviscid flow pattern inside a de-Laval convergent-divergent nozzle at design conditions is constructed numerically and the viscous shock layer in a perfect gas is solved as a two point boundary value problem iteratively.

Heat transfer, conduction, convection and radiation, are simulated next. Chemical reactions of one and several steps with several species are also discussed together with examples of chemical oscillations and chemical chaos. Finally, combustion problems are addressed including ignition models, as well as stability of solid propellant.

Part III of the book consists of short biographies of mathematicians, scientists and engineers whose works are related to the materials of the book. The Greek scholars Pythagoras, Euclid, Apollonius, Archimedes and Hero of Alexandria are among the list of mathematicians. The pioneers in this list are Descartes, Newton, Leibniz, Euler and Gauss. Also included are Pascal, Fermat, Laplace, Poisson, Fourier, D'Alembert, Lagrange, Cauchy and Poincaré from the French school, together with Huygens, Bernoulli, Riemann, Taylor, and Stokes. For scientists and engineers, the list of pioneers includes da Vinci, Copernicus, Kepler and Galileo. In fluid mechanics and aerodynamics we have Magnus, Joukowski, Prandtl, Mach, de Laval, Reynolds and Navier. In thermodynamics there are Joule, Helmholtz, Carnot, Clausius, Kelvin and Boltzman, while in heat transfer, chemical reactions and combustion there are Lavoisier, Arrhenius, Gibbs, and Maxwell. There are also, Tsiolkovsky, the father of rocketry in Russia, Hooke for Hooke's law of elastic material and Rayleigh for vibrations. These short biographies are useful to remember different aspects of the areas covered in the text.

PART I

Mathematical and Numerical Methods

2. Basic Mathematics Prerequisites

The mathematical prerequisites will cover elementary geometry, algebra and calculus. This material will be used in the numerical approximations of derivatives and integrals, and for the analytical and numerical solutions of differential equations.

2.1 Geometry

The fundamental theorem of geometry, where the distance between the two points is defined using Pythagorean theorem in 2D and 3D. Pythagoras's theorem will be used in trigonometry for calculation of the $\sin(\theta)$ and $\cos(\theta)$ as well as other related functions. We need the equations for a straight line, a circle, and other conic sections (elliptic, parabola and hyperbola). For 3D, we need the equations for planes, spheres and quadratic surfaces.

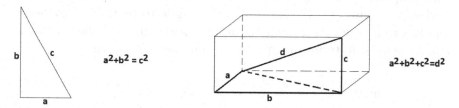

Figure 1: (*Left*) Pythagorean theorem in two dimensions. (*Right*) Pythagorean theorem in three dimensions.

2.2 Algebra

The fundamental theorem of algebra states that any polynomial of degree n has n roots counting multiplicity. We will discuss its application for the characteristic equation. In general, Newton's method is used to find the roots of polynomial equations. The fundamental theorem of linear algebra deals with existence and uniqueness for a linear system of equations $A\vec{x} = \vec{b}$, with n equations and m unknowns. If the determinant of A is nonzero (i.e. the matrix is nonsingular), then the solution is unique; otherwise there are multiple solutions, or no bounded solutions depending on conditions for $\vec{b}$. The fundamentals of matrix inverse should be covered before using the computer for matrix inversion. Examples of two equations and three equations demonstrate the details in a clear way, tridiagonal matrix will also be of particular importance. Methods to solve the linear system of equations will be compared including the inverse of A, Cramer's Rule and Gaussian Elimination. The solutions will be verified given the matrix inverse by direct multiplication. Elementary functions are discussed in detail, including polynomial, exponential, logarithmic, hyperbolic, and trigonometric, functions, as well their respective inverses. For example, the exponential function can be defined as a series given by:

$$e^x = \sum_{n=0}^{\infty} \frac{x^n}{n!}, \quad \text{where } e = \sum_{n=0}^{\infty} \frac{1}{n!} \approx 2.2.71828\ldots.$$

Notice that $e^0 = 1$, and it can be shown from calculus that a very important property of the exponential function is that the function equals its derivative at any point. This property is going to be used to evaluate the function rather than sum the infinite series. Hyperbolic functions can be defined in terms of exponential functions, for example,

$$\sinh(x) = \frac{e^x - e^{-x}}{2}, \quad \text{and} \quad \cosh(x) = \frac{e^x + e^{-x}}{2}.$$

Similarly, sine and cosine are defined in terms of e^{ix}, as given by the famous Euler formula. These elementary functions are heavily used throughout science and engineering to describe many behaviors, including growth and decay, periodicity, and their combinations.

2.3   Calculus

The concepts of continuity of functions and their limits will be summarized, including the definition of derivative and the concept of anti-derivatives. The two fundamental theorems of calculus due to Newton and Leibniz will be demonstrated. The Fundamental Theorem due to Newton is

$$\int_a^b \frac{df}{dx}dx = f(b) - f(a),$$

and the Fundamental Theorem due to Leibniz is

$$\frac{d}{dx}\int_a^x f(s)ds = f(x).$$

Repeated differentiation and integration are discussed together with geometric interpretations of first and second order derivatives (tangents to curves and curvatures), and connections with dynamics, namely velocity and acceleration in terms of displacements. Finally, derivatives and integrals of elementary functions are reviewed, together with their properties, and their approximations in terms of polynomials, for example Taylor Series. The Taylor Series is given by

$$f(x) = f(a) + f'(a)(x - a) + \frac{f''(a)}{2!}(x - a)^2 + \frac{f'''(a)}{3!}(x - a)^3 + \cdots .$$

The first several Taylor Polynomials approximating sine function, centered at $x = 0$, is given in the figure below.

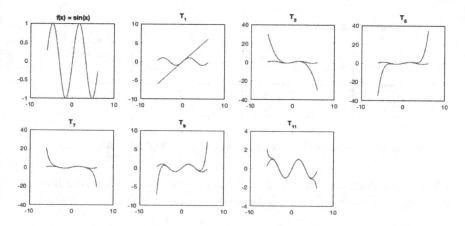

The higher order Taylor Polynomial corresponds with more terms of the Taylor Series expansion.

3. Applied Mathematics

3.1   Numerical Solutions of Algebraic Equations

For linear problems we discuss Gaussian Elimination and Cramers rule. For nonlinear problems, Newton's Method and fixed point iteration method are used.

3.1.1   *Systems of Linear Algebraic Equations*

(**2 Equations, 2 Unknowns**) Find x, y that satisfy the following system of equations by Gaussian Elimination:

$$-2x + 3y = 5$$

$$3x - y = 3.$$

We use a computer program to solve this system graphically by plotting both functions. On the other hand, we can use Gaussian Elimination and Cramer's rule to obtain the solution numerically. The relationship with the Fundamental Theorem of Linear Algebra is demonstrated with the following figure that shows the possible scenarios of two lines in the plane.

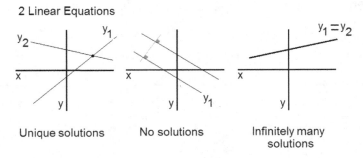

2 Linear Equations

Unique solutions   No solutions   Infinitely many solutions

We can derive Cramer's rule from applying Gaussian Elimination symbollically to two linear algebraic equations of the general form

$$ax + by = c$$

$$dx + ey = f.$$

The answer is then

$$x = \frac{det(A_1)}{det(A)}, \quad y = \frac{det(A_2)}{det(A)}$$

where

$$A = \begin{bmatrix} a & b \\ d & e \end{bmatrix}, \quad A_1 = \begin{bmatrix} c & b \\ f & e \end{bmatrix}, \quad A_2 = \begin{bmatrix} a & c \\ d & f \end{bmatrix}.$$

In the case of the example given above, the solution can then be derived as

$$A = \begin{bmatrix} -2 & 3 \\ 3 & -1 \end{bmatrix}, \quad A_1 = \begin{bmatrix} 5 & 3 \\ 3 & -1 \end{bmatrix}, \quad A_2 = \begin{bmatrix} -2 & 5 \\ 3 & 3 \end{bmatrix}$$

and thus $(x, y) = (2, 3)$. Using symbols is very important in mathematics and it is essential in computer programming. It is interesting to notice the difference between solving two equations in two unknowns by Gaussian Elimination and by inverting the matrix A. In order to find the inverse of A, which by definition is the matrix satisfying $AA^{-1} = A^{-1}A = I$, the 2×2 identity matrix. This relation gives the equations

$$AA^{-1} = \begin{bmatrix} a & b \\ d & e \end{bmatrix} \begin{bmatrix} A & B \\ D & E \end{bmatrix} = \begin{bmatrix} 1 & 0 \\ 0 & 1 \end{bmatrix}.$$

Hence there are 4 equations in 4 unknowns to solve for the matrix inverse

$$aA + bD = 1$$

$$aB + bE = 0$$

$$dA + eD = 0$$

$$dB + eE = 1.$$

These four equations are actually two decoupled sets of two equations in two unknowns. It is more expensive than solving the original two equations in two unknowns using Gaussian Elimination. With the matrix inverse the problem

$$Ax = b$$

can be formally solved by

$$x = A^{-1}b$$

which uses matrix multiplication. This choice is justifiable if we have several calculations with the same A, but different right hand side. Cramer's rule and matrix inversion for large systems of equations are computationally intensive because of the evaluation of determinants.

To demonstrate the fundamental theorem of algebra in this simple case we notice that the condition for having a unique solution is $det(A)$ is not zero, which means the system is not singular. However, if the determinant of A is zero, and the determinant of A_1 is not zero, and the determinant of A_2 is not zero, then we have two parallel lines since $a/d = b/e$ and c is different from f. It is also possible that if the $det(A)$ is zero and either the determinant of A_1 is zero or the determinant of A_2 is zero, then $a/d = b/e = c/f$ and the equations are not independent, which is to say the two equations represent the same line.

(3 Equations, 3 Unknowns) Find x, y, z that satisfy the following sysem of equations by Gaussian Elimination:

$$x - y - z = 2$$

$$x + 2y + 2z = 3$$

$$3x - 2y - 4z = 5.$$

The figures here show the 8 possible scenarios representing 3 planes in space. First there is the analog of the two-dimensional cases.

Then there is a degenerate case of one of the two-dimensional cases.

The planes can, however, intersect as follows: in 1-line, 2-lines or 3-lines.

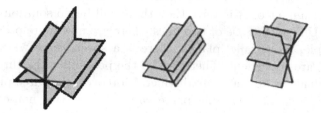

Then there is a degenerate case of intersecting in 1-line.

To explain the 8 possibilities we use Cramer's rule. Again it follows for the general case

$$a_{11}x + a_{12}y + a_{13} = b_1$$
$$a_{21}x + a_{22}y + a_{23} = b_2$$
$$a_{31}x + a_{32}y + a_{33} = b_3.$$

The answer is then

$$x = \frac{\det(A_1)}{\det(A)}, \quad y = \frac{\det(A_2)}{\det(A)}, \quad z = \frac{\det(A_3)}{\det(A)}$$

where

$$A = \begin{bmatrix} a_{11} & a_{12} & a_{13} \\ a_{21} & a_{22} & a_{23} \\ a_{31} & a_{32} & a_{33} \end{bmatrix}, \quad A_1 = \begin{bmatrix} b_1 & a_{12} & a_{13} \\ b_2 & a_{22} & a_{23} \\ b_3 & a_{32} & a_{33} \end{bmatrix},$$

$$A_2 = \begin{bmatrix} a_{11} & b_1 & a_{13} \\ a_{21} & b_2 & a_{23} \\ a_{31} & b_3 & a_{33} \end{bmatrix}, \quad A_3 = \begin{bmatrix} a_{11} & a_{12} & b_1 \\ a_{21} & a_{22} & b_2 \\ a_{31} & a_{32} & b_3 \end{bmatrix}.$$

The solution to the example problem above is $(x, y, z) = (7/3, -1/3,$ $2/3)$. If the $\det(A)$ is not zero, then there is a unique solution. Also, if the determinant of A is zero, then there will be no solution or many solutions. Unlike the case of two lines, there are now more possibilities. For example, for parallel planes, there is a special case where two of the planes are coincident. There is also the possibility the three planes are coincident, or all three are distinct. Moreover, the three planes can intersect in one line. Or one plane can intersect two non-coincident parallel planes in two lines. Or, one plane can intersect two coincident planes in one line. The last possibility is that each two planes intersect in a line and each of the lines is distinct from and parallel to the other lines. These are the 8 scenarios shown in the figures above. It is an interesting exercise to find the algebraic conditions for each scenario in terms of the determinant of the matrices A, A_1, A_2, and A_3.

3.1.2 *Nonlinear Problems*

Fixed point iteration is used for nonlinear problems, and Newton's Method is a special case. Let $f(x) = 0$, then for $\alpha \neq 0$, it follows $\alpha, f(x) = 0$, and adding x to both sides of the equation gives

$$x = x + \alpha, f(x).$$

An iteration is setup as

$$x_{\text{new}} = x_{\text{old}} + \alpha, f(x_{\text{old}}).$$

This procedure is consistent, which means that it will not change the exact solution. The convergence, if any, depends on α. The choice of

$$\alpha = -\frac{1}{\frac{df}{dx}(x_{\text{old}})}$$

is called Newton's Method. Newton's Method requires a good initial guess. Newton's Method can be derived using Taylor Series expansion around x_{old}.

$$f(x) = f(x_{\text{old}}) + \frac{df}{dx}(x_{\text{old}}) \cdot (x - x_{\text{old}}) + \cdots$$

If we require $f(x) = 0$, the above linearization will give us

$$x_{\text{new}} - x_{\text{old}} = -f(x_{\text{old}})/\frac{df}{dx}(x_{\text{old}})$$

or

$$x_{new} = x_{old} - f(x_{old}) / \frac{df}{dx}(x_{old}).$$

The geometric representation of this tangent line root formula is given in the sketch below. In particular, Newton Method is understood as replacing the function by its linearization and repeatedly solving the linear system.

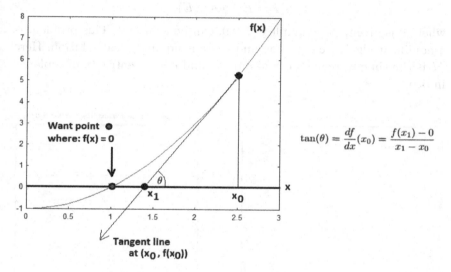

Figure 2: Newton's method iteration procedure.

A variant of Newton's Method is the secant method, given by

$$\frac{df(x_n)}{dt} \approx \frac{f(x_n) - f(x_{n-1})}{x_n - x_{n-1}}$$

and hence

$$x_{n+1} = x_n - \frac{f(x_n) \cdot (x_n - x_{n-1})}{f(x_n) - f(x_{n-1})}.$$

Thus, evaluation of derivatives is avoided. Notice the scheme needs two previous iterates to proceed, so a special treatment to start the calculation is required. The fixed point iteration can be easily extended to a system of nonlinear equations where $\vec{x}$ and $\vec{f}$ are vectors of n-components, namely

$$\vec{x}_{new} = \vec{x}_{old} + \alpha \vec{f}(x_{old}).$$

In this formula α can be a scalar, or a diagonal matrix for convenience.

3.1.3 *Kepler's Equation for Planetary Orbits*

Using Newton's Method, a solution to the algebraic equation for M and E such that

$$M = E - e\sin(E),$$

where e is given, for example $e = 0.9$, can be achieved. This problem is a nonlinear algebraic equation and there is no analytical solution. Here M is the time to reach a certain angle, and e is eccentricity of a planet in orbit.

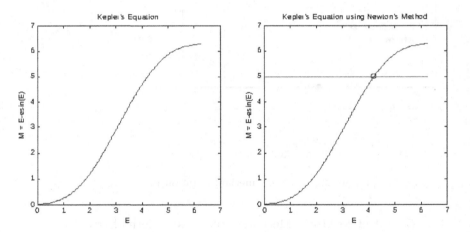

Figure 3: Kepler's equations.

3.1.4 *Root Finding and Newton Fractals*

(**Newton's Method: 2 Nonlinear Equations**) Use Newton's method to find a solution to the system of equations:

$$\frac{x^2}{a^2} + \frac{y^2}{b^2} = 1$$

$$x^2 + y^2 = 1.$$

Geometrically this problem is the intersection of a circle with an ellipse, both centered at the origin, and there can be 0, 2 or 4 solutions.

Choose $a = 2, b = 1/2$. In this case there are four possible solutions. How to find the root in the first quadrant? One strategy to solve this problem is to make an initial guess (x_0, y_0), for example $(1,1)$ and use Newton's iteration method until convergence to find the root. A different initial guess, in a different quadrant in this case, can be used to find a different root. To proceed, linearize the equations, then solve the linear system repeatedly until convergence. Notice that for polynomial equation, one can use binomial expansion instead of calculating the derivatives. The linearization is given by

$$x^2 = (x_0 + \delta_1)^2 = x_0^2 + 2\delta_1 x_0 + \delta_1^2 \approx x_0^2 + 2\delta_1 x_0$$

$$y^2 = (y_0 + \delta_2)^2 = y_0^2 + 2\delta_2 y_0 + \delta_2^2 \approx y_0^2 + 2\delta_2 y_0.$$

Linearizing x^2 and y^2 in the original equation with the above formulas, leads to 2 equations in the 2 unknowns δ_1 and δ_2.

$$\frac{1}{a^2}(x_0^2 + 2\delta_1 x_0) + \frac{1}{b^2}(y_0^2 + 2\delta_1 y_0) = 1$$

$$x_0^2 + 2\delta_1 x_0 + y_0^2 + 2\delta_1 y_0 = 1.$$

Then setting the problem up in a more classical way from linear algebra this can be written as:

$$\frac{2x_0}{a^2}\delta_1 + \frac{2y_0}{b^2}\delta_2 = 1 - \frac{x_0^2}{a^2} + \frac{y_0^2}{b^2}$$

$$2x_0\delta_1 + 2y_0\delta_2 = 1 - x_0^2 - y_0^2.$$

Note that everything is known in the above equations except the corrections δ_1 and δ_2, and that a matrix-vector form $A\vec{\delta} = \vec{b}$ is convenient for solving, by Cramer's Rule for example. Solve for the corrections. These corrections can be added to the old values to obtain the new values, and then repeat the process until convergence for $n = 0, 1, 2, \ldots$

$$x_{n+1} = x_n + \delta_1$$

$$y_{n+1} = y_n + \delta_2.$$

Notice, a single quadratic equation has two roots, two quadratic equations have four roots, three quadratic equations have eight roots, and n-quadratic equations have 2^n roots. The roots may be real or imaginary. Some of the roots may be complex conjugate pairs.

In order to use Newton's Method we need to have an initial guess for the solution, and we will obtain one root at a time by iteration. We can start the calculations with an elementary fixed point iteration where α is a constant and then switch to Newton's Method when we are closer to the root to improve the speed of convergence, since Newton's Method will be faster. In general, Gaussian Elimination is not guaranteed to work for nonlinear problems. In this particular case, it is possible to eliminate either x or y, and reduce the system to one fourth-order equation in one unknown. However, we prefer not to do that. It should be mentioned that there are solutions for 2nd, 3rd, and 4th order polynomials in closed form, but not 5th or higher. This result is called the Abel-Ruffini Theorem.

(Newton's Method: 3 Nonlinear Equations) As in the previous problem, Newton's method can be used to find a solution to a system with more coupled nonlinear equations, for example:

$$\frac{x^2}{a^2} + \frac{y^2}{b^2} + \frac{z^2}{c^2} = 1$$

$$x^2 + y^2 + z^2 = 1$$

$$\alpha x^2 - y^2 = 0.$$

Choosing $a = 2$, $b = c = 1/2$, $\alpha = 0.1$, the root in the first quadrant can be solved by using the same method as in the previous problem.

(Newton's Method: Fractals) Problems involving complex roots, like

$$z^4 = 1,$$

are a fun example to study. This problem can be reduced to two nonlinear algebraic equations in the real and imaginary part of z. However, the beauty of complex variables, is that we can apply algebraic rules to the complex numbers, hence Newton's Method can be stated for this problem in a similar form as the real case. Here where $f(z) = z^4 - 1$, Newton's Method is then

$$z_{n+1} = z_n - \frac{f(z_n)}{\frac{df}{dz}(z_n)} = z_n - \frac{z_n^4 - 1}{4z_n^3}.$$

If we choose not to use complex numbers, we can reduce the problem $z^4 = 1$ to 2 nonlinear coupled equations in the real and imaginary part of $z = x + iy$, and then apply Newton's Method to this system of equations. This approach will be more difficult. In the case of polynomial equations we use again the binomial expansion to linearize the equation, hence let's use $z_{n+1} = z_n + \delta$ where δ is a complex number representing the correction of both the real and complex part. Upon linearization,

$$z^4 = z_n^4 + 4\delta z_n^3$$

ignoring the higher order terms in δ^2, δ^3, and δ^4. The Newton's Method will give

$$4\delta z_n^3 = -(z_n^4 - 1),$$

and dividing by $4z_n^3$ gives the correction

$$\delta = -\frac{z_n^4 - 1}{4z_n^3}.$$

So, in the case of polynomials we do not have to find the derivatives explicitly.

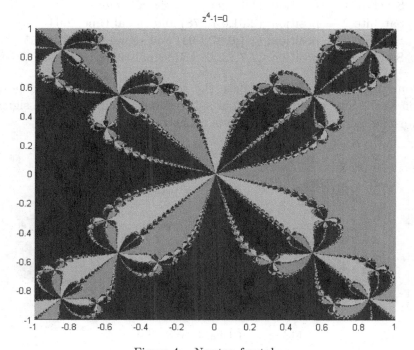

Figure 4:   Newton fractal.

Plots of the iterations needed at each grid point reveal that most points converge quadratically fast, but some do not converge and the residual error is chaotic.

3.1.5   *Global Positioning System*

An interesting application problem for Newton's Method is a simple model for a Global Position System (GPS). A basic example of how GPS works is given by using four satellites to find a position on a sphere using Newton's method. We use Newton's Method to find a global position on the unit sphere

$$x^2 + y^2 + z^2 = 1.$$

Record the satellite xyz-position and the time a signal was sent and the receiver's time. Use the time difference to calculate the signal time (in seconds). Together the data is given as

Satellite 1 — position: (1.1,1.9,0) and signal time: 21.2
Satellite 2 — position: (2.01,0,1.978) and signal time: 2.64
Satellite 3 — position: (1.1,0.97,1.04) and signal time: 32.2355
Satellite 4 — position: (1.7,1.2,0) and signal time: 18.7

From this data we can calculate the receiver's unique location position as the intersection of the four spheres associated with these signal transmission times (by radio waves which travel at light speed).

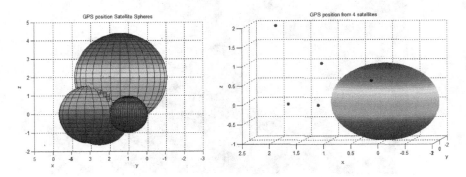

Figure 5:   Global position system.

Here the equations of the light spheres from the receiver to the satellites gives a problem of the form, find x, y, z given known positions of 1,2, and 3 satellites (x_i, y_i, z_i) and distance r_i from the receiver, such that

$$(x - x_1)^2 + (y - y_1)^2 + (z - z_1)^2 = r_1^2$$
$$(x - x_2)^2 + (y - y_2)^2 + (z - z_2)^2 = r_2^2$$
$$(x - x_3)^2 + (y - y_3)^2 + (z - z_3)^2 = r_3^2$$
$$(x - x_4)^2 + (y - y_4)^2 + (z - z_4)^2 = r_4^2$$

where $r_1 = (t_1 + \delta_1)c$, and δ is a time error due to relativity. So the 4th satellite is needed for error correction purposes due to relativistic losses, but that involves a more detailed discussion. Newton's Method is a widely used algorithm that can solve this kind of problem very quickly and it is something smartphones do nearly instantaneously billions of times a day all around the world.

3.2   Numerical Methods for Approximations of Integrals and Derivatives

In algebra, functions are studied in detail, especially lines in the plane. Lines are studied in several forms: points-slope, standard and y-intercept form. The idea of slope is emphasized and students learn to compute slope and plot lines from data points, or from equations or from a graph. In general though, mathematical functions are not all straight lines, but the question remains, is there a corresponding idea of slope, and if so, what is it, and how can it be used? The integral and differential calculus are built on the answer to this question and can be used to solve many problems involving curves and surfaces.

3.2.1   *Approximations of Integrals and Derivatives*

Archimedes was the first to solve for the area under the curve, and it was Riemann that formalized the modern technique about 2,000 years later. Let $f = f(x)$ be a smooth function as shown in the figure.

First discretize the domain into n-elements, where

$$\Delta x = \frac{x_2 - x_1}{n}.$$

At $x = x_i$, find $f(x_i) = f_i$ from the given function and connect the f_i's with straight lines (linelets). To find the integral under the graph

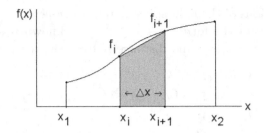

Figure 6:   Approximation of integrals.

of $f(x)$, calculate the areas of trapezoids using

$$\int_{x_1}^{x_2} f(x)dx \approx \sum_{i=1}^{n} \left(\frac{f_{i+1} + f_i}{2} \right) \Delta x.$$

Note this formula is the same as the average of the left and right rectangular rules. For better accuracy use a larger number of elements (larger n). Trapezoidal Rule can be replaced by Simpson's Rule where parabolas are fitted using three points (2 elements) instead of straight lines (linelets).

Forward, Backward and Center Difference Schemes For approximating the first derivative at i, there is Forward Difference, Backward Difference, and Center Difference rules, given by

1. Forward Difference

$$\frac{df(x_i)}{dx} \approx \frac{f_{i+1} - f_i}{\Delta x}$$

2. Backward Difference

$$\frac{df(x_i)}{dx} \approx \frac{f_i - f_{i-1}}{\Delta x}$$

3. Center Difference

$$\frac{df(x_i)}{dx} \approx \frac{1}{2}\frac{f_{i+1} - f_i}{\Delta x} + \frac{1}{2}\frac{f_i - f_{i-1}}{\Delta x} = \frac{f_{i+1} - f_{i-1}}{2\Delta x}$$

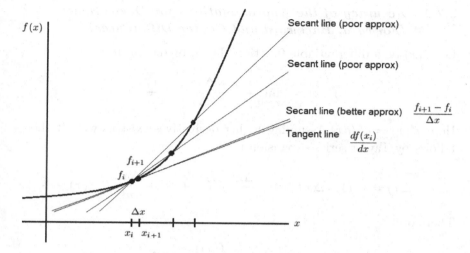

Figure 7: Geometric interpretation of finite difference as secant slope.

The last formula for Center Difference is more accurate than either Forward Difference or Backward Difference. There are also midpoint formulas

$$\frac{df(x_{i+\frac{1}{2}})}{dx} \approx \frac{f_{i+1} - f_i}{\Delta x}, \quad \text{or} \quad \frac{df(x_{i-\frac{1}{2}})}{dx} \approx \frac{f_i - f_{i-1}}{\Delta x}.$$

The second derivative (the derivative of the derivative) is

$$\frac{d^2 f}{dx^2} = \frac{d}{dx}\left(\frac{df}{dx}\right).$$

The approximation at a point x_i then gives (for uniform grid)

$$\frac{d^2 f(x_i)}{dx^2} \approx \frac{\frac{f_{i+1}-f_i}{\Delta x} - \frac{f_i-f_{i-1}}{\Delta x}}{\Delta x} = \frac{f_{i+1} - 2f_i + f_{i-1}}{\Delta x^2}.$$

This formula can be shown to be second order accurate for a uniform mesh by Taylor Series expansion, this means that the error is of order Δx^2. A first-order approximation would be expected to have error of order Δx.

3.2.2 Accuracy of the Approximations for Derivatives (Forward, Backward and Center Differences)

Let $f(x)$ be a differentiable function. Then, by definition

$$f'(x) = \lim_{\Delta x \to 0} \frac{f(x + \Delta x) - f(x)}{\Delta x}.$$

Here $f'(x) = df/dx$. Assuming higher derivatives exist as well, it then follows by Taylor series expansion that

$$f(x + \Delta x) = f(x) + \Delta x f'(x) + \frac{\Delta x^2}{2} f''(x) + \cdots + \frac{\Delta x^n}{n!} f^{(n)}(x) + \cdots.$$

Therefore

$$f'(x_i) = \frac{f(x_{i+1}) - f(x_i)}{\Delta x} + O(\Delta x).$$

A second-order central approximation of the first derivative is possible by subtracting the forward and backward differences:

$$f(x_{i+1}) - f(x_{i-1}) = f(x_i) + \Delta x_i f'(x_i) + \frac{\Delta x^2}{2} f''(x_i)$$

$$+ \cdots - \left(f(x_i) - \Delta x_i f'(x_i) + \frac{\Delta x^2}{2} f''(x_i) + \cdots \right)$$

which gives:

$$f'(x_i) = \frac{f(x_{i+1}) - f(x_{i-1})}{2\Delta x} + O(\Delta x^2).$$

A second-order central approximation of the second derivative is possible by summing the forward and backward differences:

$$f(x_{i+1}) + f(x_{i-1}) = f(x_i) + \Delta x_i f'(x_i) + \frac{\Delta x^2}{2} f''(x_i)$$

$$+ \cdots - \left(f(x_i) - \Delta x_i f'(x_i) + \frac{\Delta x^2}{2} f''(x_i) + \cdots \right)$$

which gives:

$$f''(x_i) = \frac{f(x_{i+1}) - 2f(x_i) + f(x_{i-1})}{\Delta x^2} + O(\Delta x^2).$$

To get better results from numerical methods there are typically two strategies: (1) use a finer grid, or (2) use a higher order method.

3.3 Introduction to Ordinary Differential Equations

A differential equation is a relation between a function and its derivatives. Unlike algebraic equations, where the solutions are numbers, the solutions of differential equations are functions over a domain of interest. Differential equations are widely used in science and engineering. The solution of differential equations, both analytically and numerically is a very important topic. The analytical solutions by calculus based methods are not always possible. Moreover, the solution of many differential equations by numerical methods, as will be seen below, is a relatively straightforward process that is easy to learn.

3.3.1 *Differential Equations Representing Polynomial Functions*

A good starting point is differential equations which have elementary functions as solutions. For example, one of the simplest possible differential equations is

$$\frac{du}{dt} = t^n$$

where n is an integer. The solution is a polynomial $u(t)$ which can be obtained by integration of both sides of the differential equation giving

$$u(t) = \frac{t^{n+1}}{n+1} + c$$

for some constant c. To fix the value of c, the value of $u(t)$ must be known at some time $t = t_0$. For example, if $u(0) = u_0$, then

$$u(t) = \frac{t^{n+1}}{n+1} + u_0.$$

For the special case of $n = -1$, the equation is

$$\frac{du}{dt} = \frac{1}{t}$$

and the solution is $u(t) = \ln(t) + c$. If $u(1) = 0$, the constant $c = 0$. Notice that $\ln(t)$ and e^t are inverses in the sense that $e^{\ln(t)} = \ln(e^t) = t$. Another simple example is

$$\frac{d^2u}{dt^2} = t^n$$

for some integer n. Letting $u = \frac{dv}{dt}$ and $\frac{dv}{dt} = t^n$, the solution can be obtained by integrating twice, once to get $v(t)$ and the other to get $u(t)$

$$v(t) = \frac{t^{n+1}}{n+1} + c_1$$

$$u(t) = \frac{t^{n+2}}{(n+1)(n+2)} + c_1 t + c_2.$$

Here the special cases where $n = -1$ and $n = -2$ are excluded. In this example, now two conditions are needed to determine both constants c_1 and c_2. In particular, there are two cases that should be considered separately. First, the case where these conditions are given at the same t, for example

$$u(t_0) = u_0, \quad v(t_0) = \frac{du(0)}{dt} = v_0.$$

In the second case the conditions are given on the boundaries of the domain of interest in terms of u, at the initial and final values t_i and t_f such that

$$u(t_0) = u_0, \quad u(t_f) = u_f.$$

For both cases we have to solve two algebraic equations to find the two constants using the given conditions. For the first case

$$v(0) = v_0 = c_1, \quad u(0) = u_0 = c_2$$

and the solution is

$$u(t) = \frac{t^{n+2}}{(n+1)(n+2)} + v_0 t + u_0.$$

It is easy to check that the above formula satisfies the differential equations and the given two conditions at $t = 0$. For the second case we have to solve two algebraic equations to obtain the values of c_1 and c_2, namely

$$u(t_0) = u_0 = \frac{t_0^{n+2}}{(n+1)(n+2)} + c_1 t_0 + c_2$$

$$u(t_f) = u_f = \frac{t_f^{n+2}}{(n+1)(n+2)} + c_1 t_f + c_2.$$

3.3.2 *Differential Equations Representing Exponential, Trigonometric, and Hyperbolic Functions*

The next example is more complicated since the right side is a function of u, not t. For example,

$$\frac{du}{dt} = u, \quad u(0) = u_0 = 1.$$

By inspection the solution is the exponential function

$$u(t) = e^t.$$

It is easy to check that the above solution satisfies the differential equations and the given condition at $t = 0$. Suppose now the equation is

$$\frac{du}{dt} = \alpha u, \quad u(0) = u_0.$$

Assuming a solution of the form

$$u(t) = Ae^{\lambda t}$$

by substitution into the differential equation

$$A\lambda e^{\lambda t} = \alpha A e^{\lambda t}$$

it follows that $\lambda = \alpha$ and from the condition that $u(0) = u_0$, it is determined that $A = u_0$. So the solution is found to be

$$u(t) = u_0 e^{\alpha t}.$$

If $\alpha > 0$, the solution will grow with time, while $\alpha < 0$, the solution will decay with time.

Remember the inverse of the exponential function, where t is a function of u, rather than u is a function of t, is the logarithmic function. The governing equation is given by

$$\frac{dt}{du} = \frac{1}{u}, \quad t(1) = 0.$$

In this case the solution is then $t(u) = \ln(u)$. Therefore,

$$t = \ln(u) = \ln(e^t) \quad \text{and} \quad u = e^t = e^{\ln(u)}.$$

Next consider the second order differential equation

$$\frac{d^2 u}{dt^2} = \alpha u.$$

Now two conditions given either at the same time $t = t_0$, or at two boundary times t_0 and t_f. To find the solution assume the form

$$u(t) = A e^{\lambda t},$$

and it is justifiable in this case for linear constant coefficient equations based on the properties of the exponential function. Now by substitution it is found

$$\lambda^2 A e^{\lambda t} = \alpha A e^{\lambda t},$$

hence $\lambda^2 = \alpha$. Hence $\lambda = \pm\sqrt{\alpha}$ and

$$u(t) = A_1 e^{\sqrt{\alpha} t} + A_2 e^{-\sqrt{\alpha} t}.$$

To find the constants A_1 and A_2, two algebraic equations must be solved depending on whether the two given conditions are either at the same time $t = t_0$, or at two different times t_0 and t_f. Notice that if $\alpha > 0$, the solution is in terms of two exponential functions with real exponents, while $\alpha < 0$, the solution is in terms of two exponential functions with imaginary exponents, which reduces to trigonometric functions by the Euler Formula

$$e^{it} = \cos(t) + i\sin(t).$$

For example, choosing $\alpha = 1$, the equation becomes

$$\frac{d^2u}{dt^2} - u = 0.$$

Subject to the conditions given at the same time $t = 0$

$$u(0) = 1, \quad \frac{du(0)}{dt} = 0$$

the solution is the hyperbolic cosine function $u(t) = \cosh(t)$, while for

$$u(0) = 0, \quad \frac{du(0)}{dt} = 1,$$

the solution is the hyperbolic sine function $u(t) = \sinh(t)$.

On the other hand, choosing $\alpha = -1$, the equation becomes

$$\frac{d^2u}{dt^2} + u = 0$$

and the solution subject to the conditions given at the same time $t = 0$ by

$$u(0) = 0, \quad \frac{du(0)}{dt} = 1,$$

is the sine function $u(t) = \sin(t)$, while for

$$u(0) = 1, \quad \frac{du(0)}{dt} = 0,$$

the solution is the cosine function $u(t) = \cos(t)$.

These examples from calculus are useful in the sense that we know the analytical solution *a priori*, which will be used as a check for our numerical solutions. Another way to think of these examples is to consider the properties of the elementary functions. We start with the exponential function, we know from calculus that the exponential function has a unique property, namely that the function is equal to its derivative at every point. Therefore $du/dt = u$ for any value of t. This is a first-order differential equation, and we can use this differential equation with the initial condition $u(0) = 1$ to define the exponential function. The exponential function is the unique solution of the given differential equation and the initial condition. In fact we can use the numerical solution of the differential to calculate the exponential function at any time. In this approach we used calculus, and the property of this function locally, to produce a differential equation. By choosing the initial condition we define the solution uniquely. This approach can be described as a reverse engineering process. In general, we have a differential equation, with initial (or boundary) conditions and we want to find the solution. Now we have a solution and we looked for the differential equation to describe the function. We can proceed further in this way to define trigonometry and hyperbolic functions. For example, from the properties of sine and cosine, the second derivative is equal to the negative of the original function

$$\frac{d^2 u}{dt^2} = -u.$$

We can use this differential equation together with the initial conditions $u(0) = 0, \frac{du}{dt}(0) = 1$ to define sine function as the unique solution to this differential equation. If we choose $u(0) = 1, \frac{du}{dt}(0) = 0$ the same differential equation with this new initial condition will define uniquely the cosine function. Similarly, from the property of hyperbolic functions, sinh and cosh, the second derivative is equal to the function itself

$$\frac{d^2 u}{dt^2} = u.$$

If we choose the initial condition $u(0) = 0, \frac{du}{dt}(0) = 1$, the solution of this problem will define uniquely $\sinh(t)$. On the other hand if $u(0) = 1, \frac{du}{dt}(0) = 0$, the solution of the problem will define the elementary function $\cosh(t)$. We can use this approach also to define special functions, including: Bessel function, Airy function, etc. However, in this case the differential equations are linear, but with variable coefficients.

3.3.3   *Summary of Differential Equations*

We have derived the governing equations whose solutions consist of elementary functions (polynomials, exponential, hyperbolic and trigonometric). In fact, these equations can be used to define and calculate these functions numerically. In the following modules, discussion of appropriate methods to obtain numerical solutions for these equations, as well as more general equations of similar forms without depending on analytical solutions will be given. There are four modules that will be studied in detail with many interesting applications in science and engineering.

4. Numerical Modules

4.1 Introduction to Numerical Solution of Ordinary Differential Equations

Let us start with dynamics and Newton's second law of motion $f = ma$. What is acceleration?

$$a = \frac{du}{dt}$$

where u is the velocity at each time t, and

$$u = \frac{dl}{dt}.$$

Here l is a function of time representing the distance covered in time t. Hence we have two first-order equations, together with two initial conditions

$$\frac{du}{dt} = \frac{f}{m}, \quad u(0) = u_0$$

$$\frac{dl}{dt} = u, \quad l(0) = l_0.$$

Now, if we know $l(t)$ we can proceed to find $u(t)$ by differentiation. If we know $u(t)$ we can then find $a(t)$ by differentiation, which is actually the second derivative of $l(t)$. On the other hand, if we know $a(t)$, we can find $u(t)$ by integration thanks to the fundamental theorem of calculus due to Newton. And we need the initial condition $u(0) = u_0$ to fix the constant of integration. Similarly, if we know $u(t)$ we can find $l(t)$ by integration thanks to the fundamental theorem of calculus due to Newton. Again we need the initial condition $l(0) = l_0$ to fix the constant of integration.

We can simulate this process numerically in two ways. The first approach is to replace the derivatives by differences. For example, we can write, for small Δt

$$\frac{dl}{dt} \approx \frac{\Delta l}{\Delta t}.$$

Hence, using this approximation we can replace a differential equation with discrete algebraic equations over a grid to solve for the unknowns, i.e. $l(t)$ assuming we know $u(t)$ and we have the choice of using backward difference, forward difference or trapezoidal schemes as indicated before in the section on numerical approximation of derivatives.

Alternatively we can use the integral form which is

$$l(t_2) - l(t_1) = \int_{t_1}^{t_2} u(t)dt.$$

A geometric interpretation of the Fundamental Theorem of Calculus is given in the sketch below. Note $\Delta l/\Delta t$ is an approximation of dl/dt in the element considered.

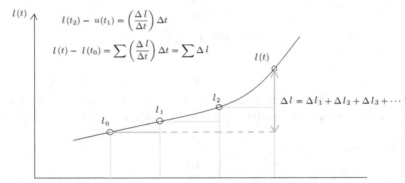

To solve the simplest example force equals mass multiplied by acceleration ($F = ma$), assuming that mass is a constant and force is given by a polynomial in time, say $F = 6t$, we integrate the equation once to get the speed, $u(t) = 3t^2$, and then again to get the distance as a function of time $l(t) = t^3$. Notice that the integration process is the reverse of the differentiation, as shown in the sketch below.

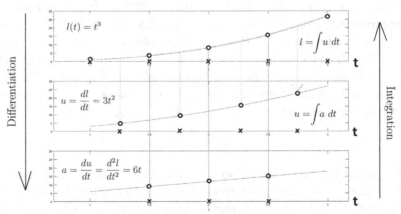

Notice we choose the grid points for the distance, speed and acceleration to make the numerical approximation second order accurate.

Another important application of calculus is related to geometry. If we have $l = l(x)$ describing a curve, the derivative dl/dx at any point represents the tangent to the curve. The second derivative d^2l/dx^2 approximately represents the curvature of a shallow curve. To show this relation we consider the curve in the figure below.

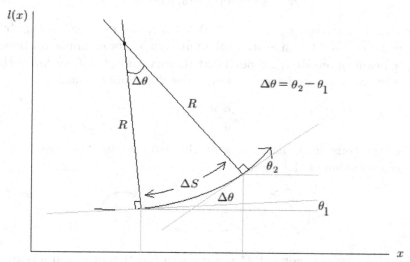

If we draw a tangent at each point and erect normals, it follows the angle between the two tangents $\Delta\theta$, and it follows that

$$R\Delta\theta = \Delta S.$$

The curvature $\kappa = 1/R$ is given by

$$\kappa = \frac{\Delta\theta}{\Delta S} \quad \text{(as } \Delta s \text{ goes to zero)}.$$

Now,

$$ds = \sqrt{dx^2 + dy^2}, \quad \tan(\theta) = \frac{dy}{dx},$$

so it follows

$$\frac{d\tan(\theta)}{d\theta}\frac{d\theta}{dx} = \frac{d^2y}{dx^2}.$$

Then using $d\tan(\theta)/d\theta = 1 + \tan^2(\theta)$

$$\frac{d\theta}{dx} = \frac{d\theta}{ds}\frac{ds}{dx} = \frac{d\theta}{ds}\sqrt{1 + (dy/dx)^2}$$

and hence

$$\frac{1}{R} = \frac{d\theta}{ds} = \frac{d^2y/dx^2}{(1 + (dy/dx)^2)^{3/2}}.$$

For a shallow curve, $(dy/dx)^2 \ll 1$, $\Delta s \approx \Delta x$, and $\kappa = 1/R \approx d^2y/dx^2$. We will use this relation in strength of materials. For example, for bending a beam, moment is proportional to curvature. So if we know the moment, M, then we have a second-order differential equation

$$C\frac{d^2y}{dx^2} = M$$

where the constant C depending on the material and the geometry of the cross-section of the beam.

Assuming that the moment M is given as a function of x, and y is given at the two ends of the domain, then we have a boundary value problem in terms of a second-order differential equation and the two boundary conditions at the ends of the domain. We can solve this problem numerically using finite difference approximations of the second derivative

$$\frac{d^2y}{dx^2} = \frac{d}{dx}\left(\frac{dy}{dx}\right) \approx \frac{\Delta\left(\frac{\Delta y}{\Delta x}\right)}{\Delta x}$$

$$= \frac{\left(\frac{y_{i+1}-y_i}{\Delta x}\right) - \left(\frac{y_i-y_{i-1}}{\Delta x}\right)}{\Delta x} = \frac{y_{i+1} - 2y_i + y_{i-1}}{\Delta x^2}.$$

If we have a beam of length L we can construct a grid from $x = 0$ to $x = L$, with N elements, where $\Delta x = L/N$, assuming the nodes are uniformly distributed, and we have the unknowns at the grid points. Applying the discrete version of the differential equation at each node gives a (tridiagonal) system of coupled algebraic equations. With the boundary values known at the first and last grid points we can use Gaussian Elimination to solve this system of equations. To find the deflection at a point x which is not a node, we can use interpolation of the values of y_i at the nodes surrounding x.

In the following, we will study four modules corresponding to four categories of problems.

1. Module 1: $\frac{du}{dt} = f(u,t)$, $u(0) = u_0$

2. Module 2: $\frac{d^2u}{dt^2} = f(u, du/dt, t)$, $u(0) = u_0$, $\frac{du(0)}{dt} = v_0$

3. Module 3: $\frac{d^2u}{dt^2} = f(u, du/dt, t)$, $u(0) = u_0$, $u(1) = u_1$

4. Module 4: $\frac{d^2u}{dt^2} + \lambda u = 0$, $u(0) = 0$, $u(1) = 0$

These forms will appear in many applications in science and engineering. In particular, it is observed that different applications may have the same underlying mathematical equation.

4.2 Module 1: Scalar First-Order Differential Equation

Considering the ideas for approximating derivatives, we have the following methods for solving differential equations of the form $du/dt = f(u,t)$.

1. Forward Difference (Explicit — First Order)

$$\frac{u_{n+1} - u_n}{\Delta t} = f(u_n, t_n)$$

2. Backward Difference (Implicit — First Order)

$$\frac{u_{n+1} - u_n}{\Delta t} = f(u_{n+1}, t_{n+1})$$

3. Trapezoidal Scheme (Implicit — Second Order)

$$\frac{u_{n+1} - u_n}{\Delta t} = \frac{1}{2}f(u_{n+1}, t_{n+1}) + \frac{1}{2}f(u_n, t_n)$$

4. Predictor-Corrector Method (Explicit — Second Order)

$$\frac{u^*_{n+1} - u_n}{\Delta t} = f(u_n, t_n)$$

$$\frac{u_{n+1} - u_n}{\Delta t} = \frac{1}{2}f(u_n, t_n) + \frac{1}{2}f(u^*_{n+1}, t_{n+1})$$

Examples: Rocket Launching, Parachute Problem, Chemical Reaction, Newton's Cooling Law, Heat Radiation

Grid: Let $t(0) = 0$, $t(n) = n\Delta t$, $n = 1, 2, 3, 4, \ldots$

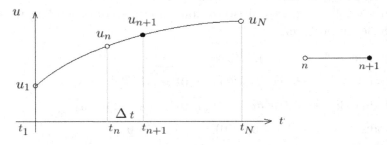

Schemes: We will consider the explicit methods only, the forward difference scheme and the predictor-corrector scheme.

1. Forward Difference
$$\frac{u_{n+1} - u_n}{\Delta t} = f(u_n, t_n), \quad n = 1, 2, 3, 4, \ldots$$

2. Predictor-Corrector
$$\frac{u_{n+1}^* - u_n}{\Delta t} = f(u_n, t_n),$$
$$\frac{u_{n+1} - u_n}{\Delta t} = \frac{1}{2}f(u_n, t_n) + \frac{1}{2}f(u_{n+1}^*, t_{n+1}), \quad n = 1, 2, 3, 4, \ldots$$

The predictor-corrector scheme is better in the sense that it is more accurate.

Solver: Explicit recursive relation: knowing, $u_0 = u(0)$, the first point exactly, solutions are then obtained by marching in time to obtain solution values $u_1, u_2, u_3, \ldots$, etc.
$$u_{n+1} = f(u_n, t_n).$$

Pseudo-code:

1. Read input and define parameters in the problem.
2. Make the grid. For example, $t = [0,\ 0.1,\ 0.2, \ldots]$. Define $\Delta t = t_{n+1} - t_n = T/N$, where T is the total elapsed time and N is the number of elements.
3. Input the initial condition to define the first value. For example $u(1) = u_1$.

4. Loop in time. For $n = 1 : N$, do $u(n+1) = \Delta t \cdot f(u_n, t_n) + u(n)$.
5. Plot $u(t)$ versus t. Label axes!

Flow Chart:

In general the code consists of three steps.

1. Discretization of the domain (grid generation),
2. Discretization of the governing differential equation (using finite difference schemes).
3. Solving the discrete algebraic equations.

4.2.1 *System of First-Order Equations*

$$\frac{d\vec{u}}{dt} = \vec{f}(\vec{u}, t), \quad \vec{u}(0) = \vec{u}_0.$$

Examples: Chemical Reactions

Schemes: Let $\vec{u} = [v, w]$, and $\vec{f} = [f_1, f_2]$. Solution by Forward Difference for $n = 1, 2, 3, 4, \ldots$

$$\frac{v_{n+1} - v_n}{\Delta t} = f_1(v_n, w_n, t_n)$$

$$\frac{w_{n+1} - w_n}{\Delta t} = f_2(v_n, w_n, t_n)$$

In this case the equations are solved by these explicit recursive relationships

$$v_{n+1} = \Delta t \cdot f_1(v_n, w_n, t_n) + v_n$$

$$w_{n+1} = \Delta t \cdot f_2(v_n, w_n, t_n) + w_n$$

The extension for n-components is straightforward. However, Forward Difference is not recommended for system of equations because it can lead to instability and so Predictor-Corrector would be used.

Examples: There is also a reduction of second-order equation to first-order system, for example Newton's second law of motion.

Schemes: Then the second-order equation can be reduced to first-order system, for example

$$\frac{dx}{dt} = v, \quad x(0) = x_0$$

$$m\frac{dv}{dt} = F \quad u(0) = \frac{dx}{dt}(0) = u_0$$

Here $\vec{u} = [x, v]$, and $\vec{f} = [v, F/m]$, and $d\vec{u}/dt = \vec{f}$, $\vec{u}(0) = (x_0, v_0)$. Then notice applying Forward Difference scheme for this case is numerically unstable, namely the error will accumulate and the calculation will blow-up. So instead, for an explicit scheme we use predictor-corrector method which is stable for small enough Δt. The issue of numerical stability will not be discussed in more depth here. Next, a single second-order equation will be considered as follows

$$\frac{d^2 x}{dt^2} = \frac{F}{m},$$

together with the two initial conditions $x(0) = x_0, v(0) = v_0$. The grid, the scheme and the solver are discussed for this problem in Module 2. Generally speaking an n-th order differential equation can be reduced to a system of n first-order equations, but not vice versa.

4.3 Module 2: Second-Order Differential Equations (Initial Value Problems)

$$\frac{d^2 u}{dt^2} = f(u, du/dt, t), \quad u(0) = u_0, \quad \frac{du}{dt}(0) = v_0.$$

Examples: Electrical Circuits, Projectiles, Orbital Mechanics, Mass-Spring-Damping Systems, Pendulum

Grid: Same as Module 1.

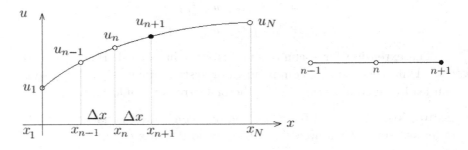

Scheme: Use central difference scheme

$$\frac{u_{n+1} - 2u_n + u_{n-1}}{\Delta t^2} = f\left(u_n, \frac{du}{dt}(t_n), t_n\right), \quad n = 2, 3, 4 \ldots .$$

This leads to the recursive relationship

$$u_{n+1} = \Delta t^2 \cdot f\left(u_n, \frac{du}{dt}(t_n), t_n\right) + 2u_n - u_{n-1}, \quad n = 2, 3, 4 \ldots .$$

For $n = 1$ use Taylor-Series Expansion

$$u_1 = u(0) + \Delta t \frac{du}{dt} + \frac{1}{2}\Delta t^2 \frac{d^2 u}{dt^2}(0).$$

Notice that the initial rate of change (for example velocity) $\frac{du}{dt}(0) = v_0$, must be given in addition to the initial point $u_0 = u(0)$. Also notice that

$$\frac{d^2(u)}{dt^2}(0) = f(u_0, v_0, t_0).$$

4.4 Module 3: Second-Order Differential Equations (Boundary Value Problems)

$$\frac{d^2 u}{dx^2} = f(u, du/dx, x), \quad u(0) = u_0, \quad u(1) = u_1.$$

Examples: Heat Conduction (Fourier Law), Flow in a Channel with Pressure Gradient, Structural Mechanics (Tension in Cables, Bending of Beams, Torsion of Shafts)

Grid: Let $x(0) = 0$. Choose the number of grid points N. Calculate Δx with $x(N) = 1$ by construction.

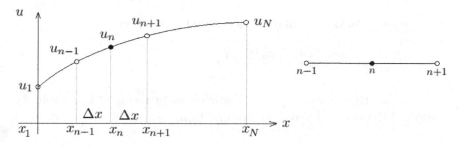

Scheme: Solution is given at $u_1 = u(0)$ and $u_N = u(1)$ and must be obtained for u_i from the solution of the discrete equations

$$\frac{u_{n+1} - 2u_n + u_{n-1}}{\Delta x^2} = f\left(u_n, \frac{du_n}{dx}, x_n\right), \quad n = 2, 3, \ldots, N-1.$$

Solver:

1. ($N = 3$), Given $u(1)$ and $u(3)$, there is only one unknown, $u(2)$ at $x = 1/2$. This case is easy to solve, since there is only one unknown and one equation.
2. ($N = 4$), Given $u(1)$ and $u(4)$, there are two unknowns, $u(2)$ at $x = 1/3$ and $u(3)$ at $x = 2/3$ and we solve two equations in two unknowns.
3. ($N = 5$), Given $u(1)$ and $u(5)$, there are three unknowns in this case, $u(2)$ at $x = 1/4$ and $u(3)$ at $x = 2/4$ and $u(4)$ at $x = 3/4$. We have now three equations in three unknowns.
4. And so on.

Alternative Case: Instead of knowing the solution values at both the left and right end points of the grid, sometimes a derivative condition is given at one of the boundaries. For example

$$\frac{d^2u}{dx^2} = f(u, du/dx, x), \quad \frac{du}{dx}(0) = c, \quad u(1) = u_1.$$

In this case a fictitious point u_0 outside of the domain is introduced. To find u_0 use the condition at $x = 0$

$$\frac{u_2 - u_0}{2\Delta x} = \frac{du}{dx}(0) = c,$$

hence, $u_0 = -2c\Delta x + u_1$ and the scheme at $x = 0$ gives

$$\frac{u_2 - 2u_1 + u_0}{\Delta x^2} = f\left(u_1, \frac{du}{dx}(x_1), x_0\right),$$

however, u_0, the fictitious point is now given in terms of the approximation of the derivative boundary condition.

4.5   Module 4: Eigenvalue Problems (Characteristic Value Problems)

Consider the problem

$$\frac{d^2u}{dx^2} + \lambda u = 0, \quad u(0) = 0, \quad u(1) = 0.$$

The exact solution is $u(x) = A\sin(\pi x)$ with $\lambda = \pi^2 \approx 9.86$. The constant A is arbitrary and can be chosen as equal to 1. Many other solutions are possible (the solution is not unique), for example $u(x) = A\sin(2\pi x)$ is also a solution.

Examples: Buckling of a Strut

Grid: Same as Module 3.

Scheme: Solution is given at $u_1 = u(0)$ and $u_N = u(1)$ and must be obtained elsewhere from the discrete equations

$$\frac{u_{n+1} - 2u_n + u_{n-1}}{\Delta x^2} + \lambda u_n = 0.$$

Solver: Find λ such that u_n is not equal to zero (this is a non-trivial solution). Then given λ generate the equations for the unknowns. Since the solution is not unique, it is possible to assume one of the unknowns is given and then calculate the others to find the (relative) shape of the buckled strut. Symmetry can also be used to save work. Example calculations are given here for several grids.

1. ($N = 3$) At the boundaries that $u_1 = u(0) = 0$ and $u_3 = u(1) = 0$. For $\Delta x = \frac{1}{2}$, the equation is

$$\frac{0 - 2u_1 + 0}{(1/2)^2} + \lambda u_1 = 0.$$

So that $-8u_1 + \lambda u_1 = u_1(\lambda - 8) = 0$, and since $u_1 \neq 0$, then $\lambda = 8$.
2. ($N = 4$) Now for $\Delta x = \frac{1}{3}$, if one assumes by symmetry that $u_2 = u_3$ then there is just a single equation to solve (instead of 2 equations),

namely,

$$\frac{u_2 - 2u_3 + 0}{(1/3)^2} + \lambda u_2 = 0.$$

So that $-9u_2 + \lambda u_2 = u_2(\lambda - 9) = 0$, and since $u_2 \neq 0$, then $\lambda = 9$. There is another interesting case with $u_2 = -u_3$, and in this case another solution is found with $\lambda = 27$.

3. ($N = 5$) Now for $\Delta x = \frac{1}{4}$, if one assumes by symmetry that $u_2 = u_4$ then there are just two equations to solve (instead of 3 equations)

$$\frac{u_2 - 2u_3 + u_2}{(1/4)^2} + \lambda u_3 = 0$$

$$\frac{u_3 - 2u_2 + 0}{(1/4)^2} + \lambda u_2 = 0$$

In matrix form this is:

$$\begin{bmatrix} -32 + \lambda & 16 \\ 32 & -32 + \lambda \end{bmatrix} \begin{bmatrix} u_2 \\ u_3 \end{bmatrix} = \begin{bmatrix} 0 \\ 0 \end{bmatrix}.$$

For u_2 and u_3 different from zero, the matrix determinant must vanish

$$\begin{vmatrix} -32 + \lambda & 16 \\ 32 & -32 + \lambda \end{vmatrix} = 0.$$

Forcing this condition gives $(-32 + \lambda)^2 = 32 \cdot 16$, which gives $\lambda \approx 9.37$. Then to find the shape of the solution, let $u_3 = 1$ and solve for u_2 using $\lambda = 9.37$ from

$$16(1 - 2u_2) + \lambda u_2 = 0,$$

to find $u_2 = u_4 = 16/(32 - 9.37) \approx 0.7070$. The exact answer is $\sin(\pi/4) \approx 0.714$.

4. ($N = 6$) and so on...

More nodes will produce more accurate solutions for the critical load as well as the shape of the strut, but it will require more work.

4.6   Numerical Stability

4.6.1   *Numerical Stability: First-Order Equations*

Besides accuracy, numerical stability is an important issue for numerical solution of differential equations. As an introduction to this idea, consider the differential equation

$$\frac{du}{dt} = -\alpha u, \quad u(0) = 1.$$

The exact solution is $u(t) = e^{-\alpha t}$. Using a forward difference approximation for du/dt, we have

$$\frac{u_{n+1} - u_n}{\Delta t} = -\alpha u_n$$

or

$$u_{n+1} = u_n - \alpha \Delta t u_n = (1 - \alpha \Delta t) u_n.$$

Hence it is observed that

$$|u_{n+1}| = |1 - \alpha \Delta t||u_n|.$$

Consider the case of $\alpha = 10$. The numerical solution will be identically zero if we choose $\Delta t = 1/\alpha = 0.1$. If we choose $\Delta t < 0.1$, the numerical solution will decay monotonically to zero. If we choose

$$|1 - \alpha \Delta t| < 1, \quad \text{or} \quad -1 < 1 - \alpha \Delta t < 1,$$

then the solution is bounded, but depending on Δt it can oscillate. If we choose $|1 - \alpha \Delta t| > 1$, the solution will blow up because of the accumulation of the errors.

In contrast to this example, consider using a backward difference approximation for du/dt

$$\frac{u_{n+1} - u_n}{\Delta t} = -\alpha u_{n+1},$$

or

$$u_{n+1} = u_n/(1 + \alpha \Delta t).$$

In this case the solution is always bounded for any choice of Δt, therefore unconditionally stable. The results for several different time steps are shown here.

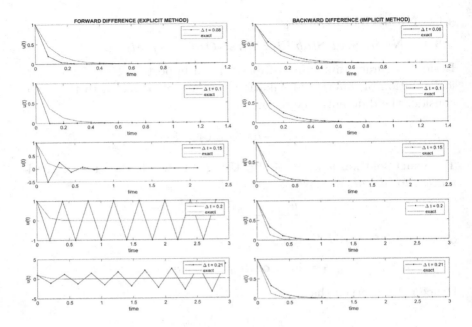

In some cases the stability requirement of simple explicit methods can be more restrictive than the accuracy requirement. Therefore there is a need for accurate stable methods, and the extra cost of implicit methods may be justifiable.

Next, consider second order schemes to solve the same problem and compare the explicit and implicit schemes based on trapezoidal scheme and predictor-corrector method. The explicit predictor-corrector scheme is given by

$$\frac{u_{n+1}^* - u_n}{\Delta t} = -\alpha u_n$$

$$\frac{u_{n+1} - u_n}{\Delta t} = -\frac{1}{2}\alpha u_{n+1}^* - \frac{1}{2}\alpha u_n$$

and the implicit trapezoidal scheme is

$$\frac{u_{n+1} - u_n}{\Delta t} = -\frac{1}{2}\alpha u_{n+1} - \frac{1}{2}\alpha u_n.$$

The numerical results are shown here.

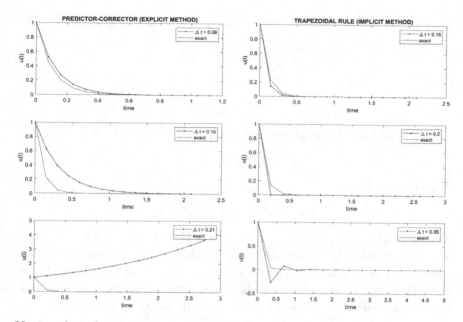

Notice that the predictor-corrector scheme can be written as

$$u_{n+1} = u_n \left(1 - \alpha\Delta t + \frac{\alpha^2\Delta t^2}{2} \right),$$

and the amplification factor, u_{n+1}/u_n, is given by the three term Taylor expansion

$$1 - \alpha\Delta t + \frac{\alpha^2\Delta t^2}{2}$$

of the exact solution value of $e^{-\alpha\Delta t}$. While for the trapezoidal scheme, the amplification factor is

$$\frac{1 - \frac{\alpha\Delta t}{2}}{1 + \frac{\alpha\Delta t}{2}}$$

which is the rational approximation of $e^{-\alpha\Delta t}$.

Notice that the 3-point central difference scheme given by

$$\frac{u_{n+1} - u_{n-1}}{2\Delta t} = -\alpha u_n,$$

is second order accurate, however, it is always unstable. To study this scheme, consider

$$u_n = \lambda^n$$

where λ is approximating $e^{-\alpha\Delta t}$. The equation for λ is given by

$$\frac{\lambda^{n+1} - \lambda^{n-1}}{2\Delta t} = -\alpha\lambda^n$$

or,

$$\lambda^{n+1} - \lambda^{n-1} + 2\Delta t\alpha\lambda^n = 0.$$

λ is governed by the quadratic equation

$$\lambda^2 + 2\alpha\Delta t\lambda - 1 = 0.$$

The solution is

$$\lambda = -\alpha\Delta t \pm \sqrt{(\alpha\Delta t)^2 + 1}.$$

So one of the $\lambda = |-\alpha\Delta t - \sqrt{(\alpha\Delta t)^2 + 1}| > 1$ and so λ^n blows up, and the solution is always unstable. Stability and accuracy are two different issues. The numerical solution confirms this result as shown here. However, to start the calculation requires a special treatment for the second point, so we used trapezoidal rule for the second point.

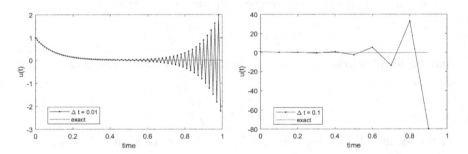

Figure 8:   (Left vs. right) For small Δt it takes more time to blow up.

4.6.2   *Numerical Stability: Second-Order Differential Equations*

Consider the linear constant coefficient equation

$$\frac{d^2u}{dt^2} + u = 0, \quad u(0) = 1, \quad \frac{du}{dt}(0) = 0.$$

The exact solution is $u(t) = \cos(t)$. Four numerical schemes will be analyzed. The cases to consider are

1. $\dfrac{u_{n+1} - 2u_n + u_{n-1}}{\Delta t^2} + u_n = 0$

2. $\dfrac{u_{n+1} - 2u_n + u_{n-1}}{\Delta t^2} + u_{n-1} = 0$

3. $\dfrac{u_{n+1} - 2u_n + u_{n-1}}{\Delta t^2} + u_{n+1} = 0$

4. $\dfrac{u_{n+1} - 2u_n + u_{n-1}}{\Delta t^2} + \dfrac{u_{n+1} + u_{n-1}}{2} = 0$

Again, assume $u_n = \lambda^n$. In all these four cases, λ^n is governed by a quadratic equation. The equations are

1. $\lambda^2 + (\Delta t^2 - 2)\lambda + 1 = 0$
2. $\lambda^2 - 2\lambda + (1 + \Delta t^2) = 0$
3. $(1 + \Delta t^2)\lambda^2 - 2\lambda + 1 = 0$
4. $(1 + \Delta t^2/2)\lambda^2 - 2\lambda + (1 + \Delta t^2/2) = 0$

From these quadratic equations the stability of each scheme is determined. The scheme is unstable if $|\lambda| > 1$. The numerical solution confirms that the first scheme is conditionally stable, the second is always unstable, and the third and fourth are unconditionally stable. The instability of the second scheme is shown in the figure below.

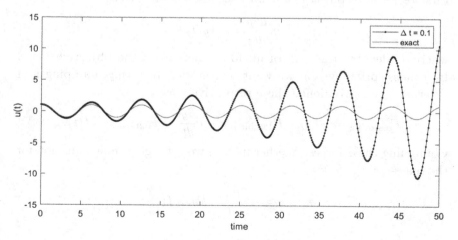

Figure 9: $\dfrac{u_{n+1} - 2u_n + u_{n-1}}{\Delta t^2} + u_{n-1} = 0$.

As far as accuracy is concerned, the first and the fourth are second order accurate, while the second and third are first order accurate. So the fourth scheme, which is second order accurate and always stable is the best one.

5. Numerical Solution of Differential Equations

In this section we will consider linear differential equations with constant and variable coefficients, as well as nonlinear differential equations. Scalar and systems, and homogeneous and non-homogeneous problems will be considered. We will use simple uniform grids, and the schemes of the modules discussed in Section 4 to solve this wide variety of mathematical problems. In Part II, applications in science and engineering will follow using the same strategy.

5.1   Linear Differential Equations with Constant Coefficients

5.1.1   *Mass-Spring System*

First recall from physics Newton's second law of motion

$$m\frac{d^2y}{dt^2} = F(y, t)$$

where F denotes the sum of all forces acting on the objective mass. In a mass-spring system we want to consider: restoring, damping and external forces. We define these respectively as:

$$F_{\text{restoring}} = -ky, \quad F_{\text{damping}} = -c\frac{dy}{dt}, \quad F_{\text{external}} = f(t).$$

Combining these forces together in $F(t)$ we get a governing equation for the mass-spring system

$$m\frac{d^2y}{dt^2} = -c\frac{dy}{dt} - ky + f(t)$$

which is typically rearranged in the classical way

$$m\frac{d^2y}{dt^2} + c\frac{dy}{dt} + ky = f(t).$$

It is a second order, constant coefficient, non-homogeneous linear differential equation. Physically, one may consider the cases: $m > 0, k > 0$, $c \geq 0$. Mathematically, one can consider other parameter values. Additionally, m, c, k can all be considered as functions of time and this leads to interesting examples. If $f(t) = 0$, the dynamics are unforced, we then say it is homogeneous.

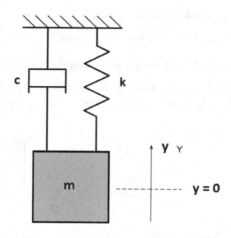

Figure 10:   Damped forced oscillator.

In modeling vibration of building foundations, vehicle suspension, seismometers and accelerometers, a damped forced vibration arises. In the event some vibration motion is forcing the system, the model becomes a forced-mass-spring system of the form

$$m\frac{d^2y}{dt^2} + ky + c\frac{dy}{dt} = \text{vibration force}.$$

The vibration force can take many forms depending on the source. It is essential to first understand what is called harmonic forcing. In this case the equation of motion becomes

$$m\frac{d^2y}{dt^2} + c\frac{dy}{dt} + kx = a\sin(\omega t)$$

for a constant value a.

5.1.2 *Stability Analysis for Mass-Spring System*

For homogeneous system when $f(y,t) = 0$, assuming a solution of the form $y = e^{\lambda t}$ it follows

$$m\lambda^2 + c\lambda + k = 0.$$

The quadratic equation, has the solutions

$$\lambda_{1,2} = \frac{-c \pm \sqrt{c^2 - 4mk}}{2m}.$$

There are three cases

$c^2 > 4mk$ Overdamped: Distinct real roots $(\lambda_{1,2})$

$c^2 = 4mk$ Critically damped: Real repeated roots $(\lambda_1 = \lambda_2)$

$c^2 < 4mk$ Underdamped: Complex conjugate roots $(\lambda_{1,2} = \alpha \pm i\beta)$

The physical meaning of overdamped, critically damped and underdamped is related to how the mass returns to equilibrium.

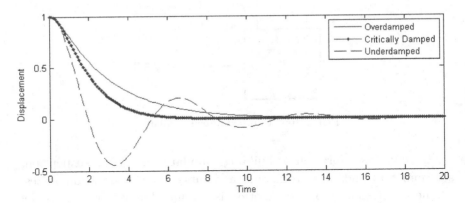

Figure 11: Mass spring system root cases.

The quadratic equation is called the characteristic equation, where λ is called the characteristic value (or eigenvalue). Examining the solution of this problem it is clear from the formula for the roots of the characteristic equation the dependence of the solution on the parameters m, c, k which represent mass, damping and the spring constant, respectively. We assume mass, m, is always positive. In these cases the stability can be determined from the coefficients $K = k/m$ and $C = c/m$.

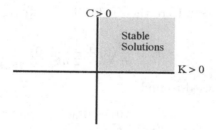

Figure 12: Mass-Spring-Damping system stable solutions. $K > 0$ is static stability (spring with restoring force). Here if $C > 0$ means dynamic stability (damping resisting the motion).

By stability, we mean bounded input produces bounded output.

5.1.3 Scalar Non-Homogeneous Damped Mass Spring System

First let $f(t) = 10\cos(3t)$, $m = 1$, $c = 4$, and $k = 5$ to get a differential equation of the form:

$$\frac{d^2y}{dt^2} + 4\frac{dy}{dt} + 5y = 10\cos(3t)$$

subject to the initial conditions:

$$y(0) = 0, \quad y'(0) = 0.$$

Use $h = \Delta t = 0.1$ and solve out to time $t = 2$. To check your answers the true solution is given by:

$$y(t) = e^{-2t}\left(\frac{1}{4}\cos(t) - \frac{7}{4}\sin(t)\right) - \frac{1}{4}\cos(3t) + \frac{3}{4}\sin(3t).$$

We will implement finite difference methods to numerically solve this initial value problem. To solve the general equation we can discretize the system as

$$m\frac{y_{n+1} - 2y_n + y_{n-1}}{\Delta t^2} + c\frac{y_{n+1} - y_{n-1}}{2\Delta t} + ky_n = f(t_n).$$

Notice y_0 is given. To find y_1 use Taylor Series expansion and the initial conditions for y_0 and the derivative $\frac{dy}{dt}(0)$ as well as the differential equation itself at $t = 0$. Here the Taylor Series expansion is

$$y_1 = y_0 + \frac{dy}{dt}(0) + \frac{1}{2}\frac{d^2y}{dt^2}(0)$$

which can then be used to find

$$y_1 = \frac{10\cos(3t_0)}{2/(\Delta t)^2}.$$

The values for y_2, y_3 and so on can be obtained from the recursive relation, since y_{n+1} is related to y_n, and y_{n-1}. Notice in the numerical methods to solve the non-homogeneous linear differential equations there is no need to decompose the solution to homogeneous (transient) and non-homogenous (steady state) components.

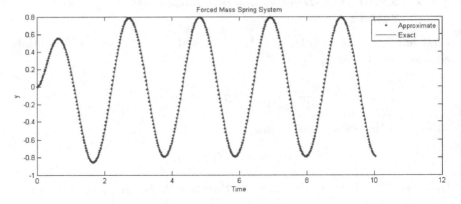

Figure 13:   Classical mass-spring-system.

This is an example of a classical damped forced mass-spring system. Several other interesting examples are available. The case of beats and pure resonance are of particular interest.

5.1.4   *Pure Resonance*

In the case of pure resonance we have the natural frequency of the system matching the frequency of the forcing function. In this case oscillations in the solutions are self-reinforcing and the solution amplitude grows in time. An example of this phenomenon is:

$$\frac{d^2y}{\Delta t^2} + y = 2\cos(t), \quad y(0) = 0, \quad y'(0) = 0.$$

Here, discretize this equation as above and numerically solve it. Use $h = 0.5$ and solve to $t = 10$. To check your answer use:

$$y(t) = c_1\cos(t) + c_2\sin(t) + t\sin(t) = t\sin(t)$$

$$c_1 = c_2 = 0 \text{ from the initial conditions}$$

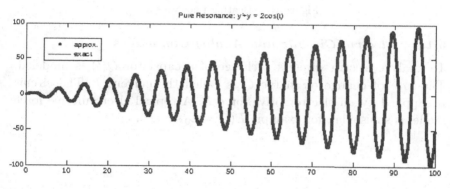

Figure 14:   Resonance.

5.1.5   *Beating Phenomena*

The case of beats is related to the phenomenon of amplitude modulation. Here we will consider:

$$m\frac{d^2y}{dt^2} + ky = F_0\cos(\omega t), \quad y(0) = 0, \quad y'(0) = 0.$$

Next discretize this equation as above and solve it numerically. Use $h = 0.001$ and numerically solve to $t = 50$ with $m = 1$, $k = 3$, $F_0 = 1$, $\omega = 2$, and $\omega_0 = \sqrt{k/m}$. Experiment with how much accuracy you lose with a large step size. The answer can be checked with the exact solution

$$y(t) = \frac{F_0}{m(\omega_0^2 - \omega^2)}(\cos(\omega t) - \cos(\omega_0 t)).$$

Note that because of the highly oscillatory nature of this problem a very fine discretization is required to get accurate results. This is a common and important issue of resolution for multiple time scale problems.

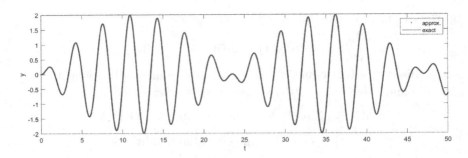

Figure 15:   Beating phenomena.

5.1.6   *Electric Circuits and Analog Computers*

To analyze electric circuits a charge of a capacitor $Q(t)$ is modeled. The rate of change of charge Q is called the current I. The circuit is supplied by an electromotive force E. A typical electromotive force model is sinusoidal, for example $E(t) = E_0 \sin(\omega t)$.

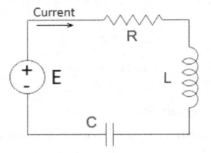

The circuit also contains an Ohm's Resistor, R, Inductor L and Capacitor C. A second order equation can be derived from Kirchhoff's Law to model these components in series around a circuit by

$$L\frac{d^2Q}{dt^2} + R\frac{dQ}{dt} + \frac{1}{C}Q = E(t)$$

subject to the initial conditions

$$Q(0) = Q_0, \quad Q'(0) = I(0) = I_0.$$

Note that $I = dQ/dt$, and hence by differentiation of the above equation we have

$$L\frac{d^2I}{dt^2} + R\frac{dI}{dt} + \frac{1}{C}I = E'(t).$$

In the special case of an RC-Circuit (where $L = 0$), a first order model for current due to the electromotive force as a function of time is given by

$$R\frac{dI}{dt} + \frac{1}{C}I = \frac{dE}{dt}, \quad I(0) = c$$

where c is the initial current. There is an analogy between the circuit and the Mass-Spring System where: displacement is charge, velocity is current, mass is inductance, damping is resistance, spring constant is elastance $(1/C)$, and external forcing is electromotive forcing.

Translational	**Rotational**	**Electrical**
Force (f)	Torque (T)	Voltage (v)
Mass (M)	Inertia (J)	Inductance (L)
Damper (D)	Damper (D)	Resistance (R)
Spring (K)	Spring (K)	Elastance $(1/C)$
Displacement (x)	Displacement (Θ)	Charge (q)
Velocity $(u) = \dot{x}$	Velocity $(u) = \dot{\theta}$	Current $(i) = \dot{q}$

Consider the first-order differential equation for the current $I(t)$

$$\frac{dI}{dt} + 3I = 15,$$

subject to the initial condition $I(0) = 0$. The exact solution is

$$I(t) = 5 - 5e^{-3t}.$$

Shown below is the numerical solution for the current as a function of time.

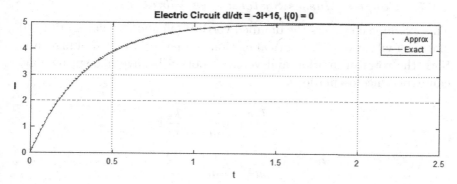

Next consider the second-order differential equation for the charge $Q(t)$

$$\frac{d^2Q}{dt^2} + 40\frac{dQ}{dt} + 625Q = 100\cos(10t),$$

subject to the initial conditions $I(0) = 0$ (*Note: $I = dQ/dt$*) and $Q(0) = 0$. The exact solution is

$$Q(t) = \frac{4}{697}\left(\frac{-e^{-20t}}{3}(63\cos(15t) + 116\sin(15t))\right.$$

$$\left. + 21\cos(10t) + 16\sin(10t)\right).$$

Shown below is the numerical solution for the charge as a function of time.

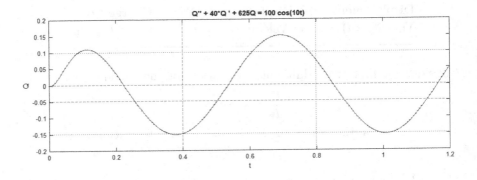

5.1.7   *Coupled Masses System: Free Vibration*

This example considers the damped vertical (x) and angular motion (θ) of a wing vibration. The vertical motion is sometimes called plunge, and both the rotation motion and vertical motion behave like springs and can experience oscillations.

$$\frac{d^2x}{dt^2} - e\frac{d^2\theta}{dt^2} + \frac{k_1}{m}x = 0$$

$$(e^2 + J/M)\frac{d^2\theta}{dt^2} - e\frac{d^2x}{dt^2} + \frac{k_2}{m}\theta = 0$$

To solve this coupled system of differential equations first discretize the equations.

$$\frac{x_{n+1} - 2x_n + x_{n-1}}{\Delta t^2} - e\frac{\theta_{n+1} - 2\theta_n + \theta_{n-1}}{\Delta t^2} + \frac{k_1}{m}x_n = 0$$

$$(e^2 + J/M)\frac{\theta_{n+1} - 2\theta_n + \theta_{n-1}}{\Delta t^2} - e\frac{x_{n+1} - 2x_n + x_{n-1}}{\Delta t^2} + \frac{k_2}{m}\theta_n = 0.$$

Now the differential equations have been reduced to a coupled system of algebraic equations. This is the framework the problem will be solved from, but it is convenient to proceed as follows. First consider re-writing the differential equation in the form:

$$B = -e/(e^2 + J/m)$$

$$x'' - A\theta'' = -(k1/m)x$$

$$\theta'' + Bx'' = -(k2/m)1/(e^2 + J/M)\theta.$$

From the following definitions,

$$C = -(k1/m)x_n$$

$$D = -(k2/m)1/(e^2 + J/M)\theta_n$$

the equations can be written as

$$x'' - A\theta'' = C$$

$$\theta'' + Bx'' = D.$$

Now by using algebra solve for

$$x_{n+1} - A\theta_{n+1} = 2x_n - x_{n-1} + A(-2\theta_n + \theta_{n-1}) + \Delta t^2 C = F$$

$$B(x_{n+1} + \theta_{n+1}) = 2\theta_n - \theta_{n-1} - B(-2x_n + x_{n-1}) + \Delta t^2 D = G.$$

With our F, G for the right-hand side terms, the equations can be written in the form:

$$x_{n+1} - A\theta_{n+1} = F$$

$$-Bx_{n+1} + BA\theta_{n+1} = -BF.$$

The solution of this system of linear algebraic equations is

$$x_{n+1} = (AG + F)/(1 + AB)$$

$$\theta_{n+1} = (G - BF)/(BA + 1).$$

Choosing $e = -0.2$, $m = 1$, $J = 2$, $k_1 = 0.4$, $k_2 = 1$ produces the following periodic motion.

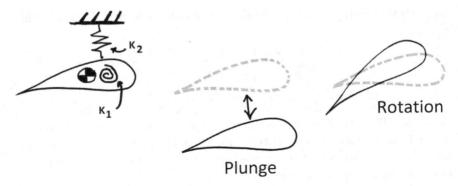

Figure 16:   An airfoil, with two modes of motion: rotation (θ) and plunge (x). Each motion is modeled by a spring.

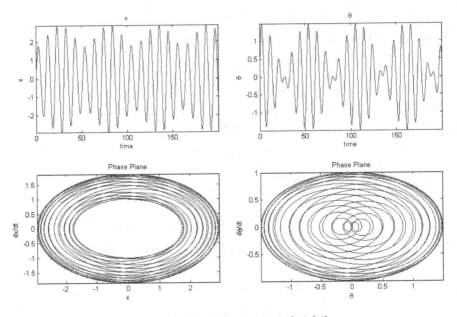

Figure 17:   Periodic motion of airfoil.

5.1.8   *Coupled Damping System: Brouwer's Gyroscopic Effect*

Brouwer's rotating particle problem is derived from considering the motion of a heavy particle inside a rotating vessel. This model is used to study gyroscopic stabilization. The governing equations are given by[2]

$$\frac{d^2x}{dt^2} - 2\Omega\frac{dy}{dt} + (k_1 - \Omega^2)x = 0$$

$$\frac{d^2y}{dt^2} + 2\Omega\frac{dx}{dt} + (k_2 - \Omega^2)y = 0$$

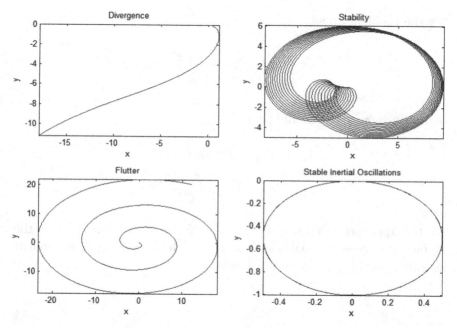

Figure 18:   Brouwer's gyroscopic effect.

Here the problem is solved for several cases. To see divergence set $k_1 = 0.25$, $k_2 = -0.3$, $\Omega = 0.4$, and solve for $0 \leq t \leq 8$. To see stable cycles set $k_1 = 0.25$, $k_2 = -0.3$, $\Omega = 0.6$, and solve for $0 \leq t \leq 8$. To see flutter, in which the instability gradually increases, set $k_1 = 0.25$, $k_2 = -0.3$, $\Omega = 0.9$, and solve for $0 \leq t \leq 8$. To see stable inertial oscillations set $k_1 = 1$, $k_2 = 1$, $\Omega = 1$, and solve for $0 \leq t \leq \pi$. To solve any of these

---

[2]Kirillov, O.N. *Nonconservative Stability Problems of Modern Physics*. De Gruyter Studies in Mathematical Physics (2013).

problems discretize the equations as usual

$$\frac{x_{n+1} - 2x_n + x_{n-1}}{\Delta t^2} - 2\Omega\frac{y_{n+1} - y_{n-1}}{2\Delta t} + (k_1 - \Omega^2)x_n = 0$$

$$\frac{y_{n+1} - 2y_n + y_{n-1}}{\Delta t^2} + 2\Omega\frac{x_{n+1} - x_{n-1}}{2\Delta t} + (k_2 - \Omega^2)y_n = 0.$$

Set the problem up as

$$x_{n+1} - Cy_{n+1} = E$$
$$y_{n+1} + Cx_{n+1} = F$$

and then show algebraically that

$$x_{n+1} = (E + CF)/(1 + C^2)$$
$$y_{n+1} = -\frac{E/C - (E + CF)}{C + C^3}$$

for the appropriate choice of $C, E,$ and F. A longer time plot of the stable case, when $\Omega = 0.6$ is shown along with the x and y displacement as a function of time up to $t = 1000$.

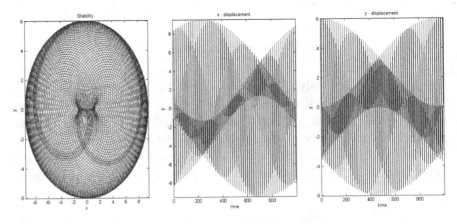

Figure 19: Stable case in gyroscopic motion.

5.1.9   *Coupled Stiffness System: Landing Gears*

This example considers two masses coupled by springs to make a simple model of landing gear response during landing.

$$m_1 \frac{d^2 x_1}{dt^2} + (k_1 + k_2)x_1 - k_2 x_2 = 0$$

$$m_2 \frac{d^2 x_2}{dt^2} - k_2 x_1 + k_2 x_2 = 0$$

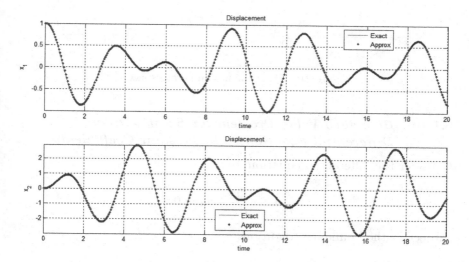

Figure 20:   Landing gear.

The solution is achieved by discretization as usual

$$m_1 \frac{x_1(n+1) - 2x_1(n) + x_1(n-1)}{\Delta t^2} + (k_1 + k_2)x_1(n) - k_2 x_2(n) = 0$$

$$m_2 \frac{x_2(n+1) - 2x_2(n) + x_2(n-1)}{\Delta t^2} - k_2 x_1(n) + k_2 x_2(n) = 0$$

and then solving algebraically for

$$x_1(n+1) = 2x_1(n) - x_1(n-1) - \Delta t^2((k_1 + k_2)x_1(n) - k_2 x_2(n))/m_1$$
$$x_2(n+1) = 2x_2(n) - x_2(n-1) - \Delta t^2(-k_2 x_1(n) + k_2 x_2(n))/m_2.$$

In the case of coupled second order system of equations it is useful to plot the phase planes and state space. The x_1 and x_2 phase planes are: x_1 by dx_1/dt, and x_2 by dx_2/dt. The state space is x_1 by x_2.

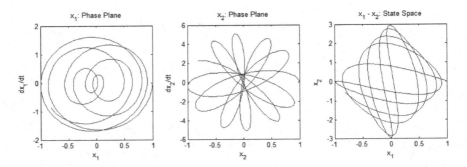

Figure 21: Phase planes and state space.

5.1.10 *Boundary Value Problem for Second-Order Differential Equation with Constant Coefficients*

Consider the differential equation:

$$\frac{d^2u}{dx^2} + a\frac{du}{dx} + bu = 0$$

subject to the boundary conditions

$$u(0) = 1 \quad \text{and} \quad u(1) = c = 4.$$

The exact solution is

$$u(x) = Ae^{m_1 x} + Be^{m_2 x}$$

where m_1 and m_2 are the roots of the quadratic equation

$$m^2 + am + b = 0.$$

Choose $a = 2$ and $b = -3$, and hence $m_1 = 1$ and $m_2 = -3$. Now, $1 = A + B$ and $c = A\exp(1) + B\exp(-3)$ or, $c = A\exp(1) + (1 - A)\exp(-3)$

for $c = 4$. Solve for A and hence $B = 1 - A$. Here we compare the exact solution with the numerical solution following module 3.

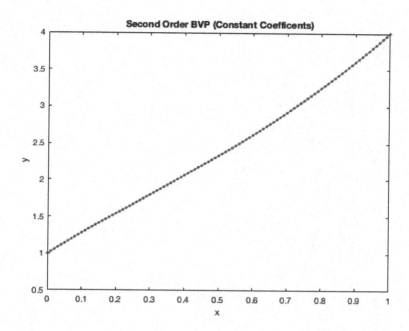

Next we solve a problem with derivative boundary conditions for

$$\frac{d^2y}{dx^2} + \frac{dy}{dx} + 0.25y = 0,$$

now using $y(0) = 3$, $\frac{dy(0)}{dx} = -3.5$. Here the discretization is again

$$\frac{y_{n+1} - 2y_n + y_{n-1}}{\Delta x^2} + \frac{y_{n+1} - y_{n-1}}{2\Delta x} + 0.25y_n = 0.$$

In this case, the exact solution is

$$y = (c_1 + c_2 x)e^{-0.5x}$$

with $c_1 = 3$, $c_2 = -2$. The numerical solution is in good agreement with the exact solution as shown in the figure below.

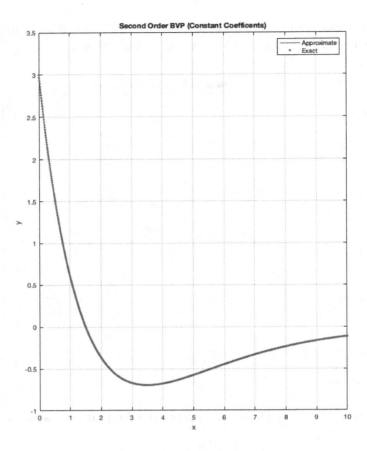

5.1.11 *Second-Order Equation with Small Parameter*

What happens to the solution when the coefficient of the second-order derivative is a small parameter ϵ? For example, consider

$$-\epsilon \frac{d^2 u}{dx^2} + u = 1.$$

In this case, suppose we enforce boundary values such as $u(0) = 0$ and $u(1) = 0$, or $u(1) = 2$. For sufficiently small epsilon one expects the solution to look like $u = 1$, but this would not satisfy the boundary conditions. Therefore, there must be a smooth transition from $u = 1$ that also satisfies the boundary conditions. This is the concept of boundary layer where there is a smooth large gradient region near the boundary to satisfy the boundary condition. Here the exact solution is

$$u = Ae^{-x/\sqrt{\epsilon}} + Be^{x/\sqrt{\epsilon}} + 1.$$

The numerical solution for $\epsilon = 0.01$ is shown below.

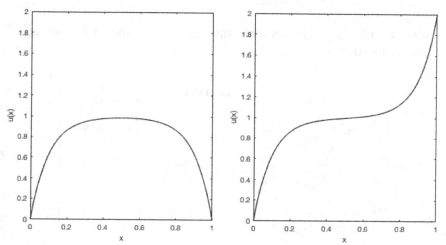

5.2 Linear Differential Equations with Variable Coefficients

5.2.1 *Example of First-Order Differential Equation*

An example of a variable coefficient problem is

$$\frac{dy}{dx} = -2xy, \quad y(0) = 1.$$

The analytic solution is given by the Gaussian distribution

$$y = e^{-x^2}.$$

If we use the most convenient method (Forward Euler), the difference equation would be given by

$$\frac{y_i - y_{i-1}}{\Delta x} = -2x_i y_i.$$

To improve the situation, midpoint or trapezoidal rule can be used to get a more accurate solution. In this case, the trapezoidal rule is given by

$$\frac{y_i - y_{i-1}}{\Delta x} = -2 \left(\frac{x_i y_i + x_{i-1} y_{i-1}}{2} \right).$$

Forward Euler and Trapezoidal Rule results are shown in the figure compared with the analytical solution.

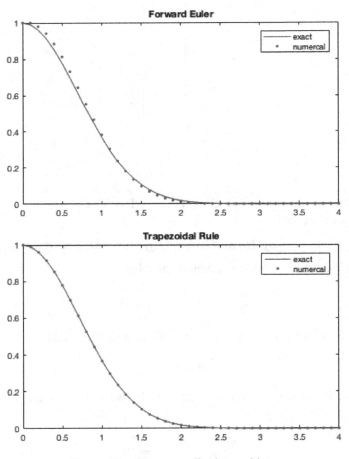

Figure 22:   Linear coefficient problem.

5.2.2 *Bessel Functions of the First Kind*

So far only elementary functions are studied. Special functions are also introduced through differential equations. For example Bessel's differential equation is given by

$$y'' + \frac{1}{x}y' + \left(1 - \frac{\nu^2}{x^2}\right)y = 0, \quad \nu \geq 0.$$

For $\nu = 0$ consider Bessel D.E. subject to $y(0) = 1, y'(0) = 0$, and for $\nu = 1$ also consider Bessel D.E. subject to $y(0) = 0, y'(0) = 1/2$. The solutions can be compared with

$$y_0 \approx 1 - \frac{x^2}{2^2(1!)^2} + \frac{x^4}{2^4(2!)^2} - \frac{x^6}{2^6(3!)^2} + \cdots$$

and

$$y_1 \approx \frac{x}{2} - \frac{x^3}{2^3(1!2!)} + \frac{x^5}{2^5(2!3!)} - \frac{x^7}{2^7(3!4!)} + \cdots$$

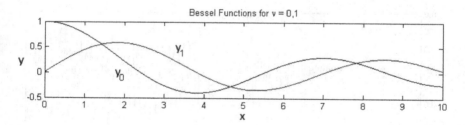

Figure 23:   Bessel functions.

5.2.3 *Airy Functions*

Another example of a special function is given by the following Airy equation

$$\frac{d^2y}{dx^2} - xy = 0.$$

Here define Ai by $y(0) = 0.35503$, and $y'(0) = -0.25882$, and define Bi by $y(0) = 0.61493$, and $y'(0) = 0.44829$. The solutions are given in the following figure.

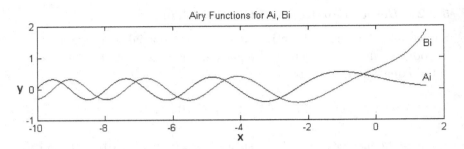

Figure 24:   Airy functions.

5.2.4   *Mathieu Equation*

The Mathieu equation is a two parameter second-order linear equation describing frequency modulation, with many applications in engineering, especially dynamics, and is given by:

$$u'' + (w_0^2 + \epsilon w_1^2 \cos(w_1 t))u = 0.$$

Similar to the resonance phenomenon this equation can exhibit blow-up.

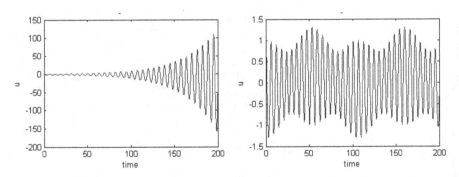

Figure 25:   Mathieu equation example solution with blow-up (*left*) compared with an example solution that remains bounded (right).

The next plot indicates the boundary between regions where the maximum value of $u(t)$ is finite, or tending to infinity. Each point on the plot corresponds with a solution for $u(t)$ depending on ε and $w_0^2/w1^2$.

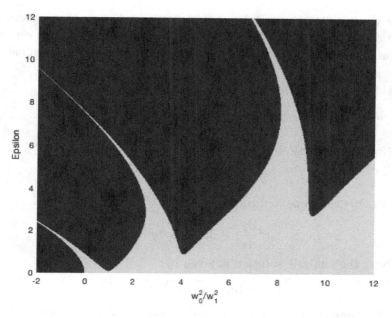

Figure 26:   Mathieu equation.

To reproduce this result, start with an initial solution and color the solution based on whether the function $u(t)$ remains bounded by some appropriately large value, or exceeds that value. Some tuning may be required, as well as careful choice of the grid in time. Note that the equation must be integrated many times for the different parameter values, in two nested loops.

5.2.5 *Euler–Cauchy Equation*

The second order Euler–Cauchy equation appears in a number of applications, particularly in polar coordinates. In general, it is a linear homogeneous ordinary differential equation with variable coefficients of order n:

$$f_n(x)\frac{dy^n}{dx^n} + \cdots + f_1(x)\frac{dy}{dx} + y_0 f_0(x) = 0.$$

First we will consider a special case where:

$$x^2\frac{dy^2}{dx^2} + ax\frac{dy}{dx} + by = 0.$$

Here we pay attention to the root structure and how that affects the solution. We will study three cases: (1) two distinct roots, (2) one real repeated root, and (3) complex roots, depending on the choice of parameters [see Kreyzig].

(1) Two distinct roots (m_1, m_2)

$$x^2 \frac{dy^2}{dx^2} - \frac{5}{2} x \frac{dy}{dx} - 2y = 0.$$

Now the analytic solution is given by:

$$y(x) = c_1 x^{m_1} + c_2 x^{m_2}.$$

(2) One real repeated root

$$x^2 \frac{dy^2}{dx^2} - 3x \frac{dy}{dx} + 4y = 0.$$

Now the analytic solution is given by:

$$y(x) = (c_1 + c_2 \ln(x)) x^{(1-a)/2}.$$

(3) Complex conjugate roots $(m_1 = \mu + i\nu, m_2 = \mu - i\nu)$

$$x^2 \frac{dy^2}{dx^2} + 7x \frac{dy}{dx} + 13y = 0.$$

Now the analytic solution is given by:

$$y(x) = x^{\mu} [A \cos(\nu \ln(x)) + B \sin(\nu \ln(x))].$$

In addition we also want to consider a non-homogeneous case:

$$x^2 \frac{dy^2}{dx^2} - 4x \frac{dy}{dx} + 6y = -7x^4 \sin(x).$$

Here the analytic solution is given by:

$$y(x) = c_1 x^2 + c_2 x^3 + 7x^2 \sin(x).$$

For each of the above problems we used $y(1) = 1$, $\frac{dy}{dx}(1) = 1$ and solve the equations numerically. The constants c_1 and c_2 are found by imposing the initial conditions in order to compare the numerical results to the analytical solutions. In the figure below, the numerical results together with the analytical solution to the following problem are plotted.

$$x^2 y'' + 1.5xy' - 7.5y = 0, \quad y(1) = 0, \quad \frac{dy}{dx}(1) = 1.$$

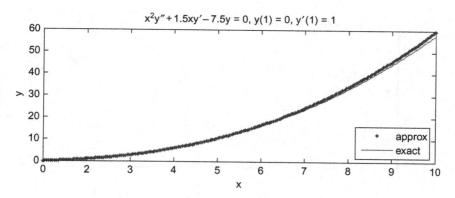

Figure 27:   Cauchy Euler equations.

The exact solution in this case is $y(x) = \frac{2}{11}x^{5/2} - \frac{2}{11}x^{-3}$.

Another variation of this example is given by

$$x^2y'' + axy'\frac{1}{4}(1-a)^2y = 0, \quad y(0.5) = x^m, \quad \frac{dy}{dx}(0.5) = mx^{m-1}$$

with $a = 1 - 2m$. The exact solutions are given by $y = x^m$. Solutions for real distinct roots is shown here.

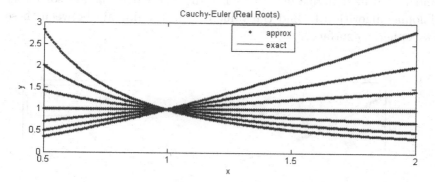

Figure 28:   Real distinct roots.

In the case of complex roots the solution curves are shown below.

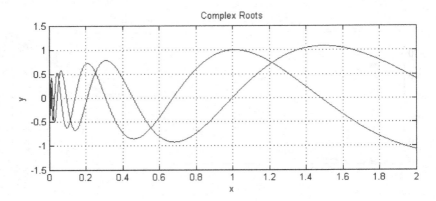

Figure 29:   Complex roots.

Another example, where the boundary values are given instead of initial values, requires the numerical solution using the Thomas algorithm (see the Appendix). In this case we consider differential equation given by

$$rv'' + 2v' = 0$$

with known values of $v = 110$ on a spherical surface of radius $r = 4$ and $v = 0$ at a radius of $r = 8$. The discrete equations are solved by Thomas algorithm to find the value of v in the domain between these two spherical surfaces.

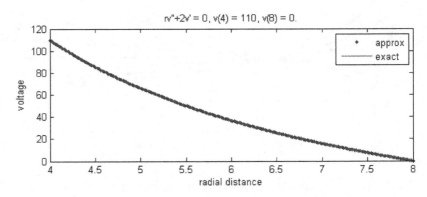

Figure 30:   Euler–Cauchy equations: Voltage between spheres.

The exact solution is given by $v(r) = -110 + 880/r$.

5.2.6 *Legendre Polynomials*

Legendre functions are solutions to Legendre's differential equation:

$$\frac{d}{dx}\left[(1-x^2)\frac{d}{dx}P_n(x)\right] + n(n+1)P_n(x) = 0.$$

Here, we solve the boundary value problem subject to the boundary conditions:

$$y(1) = 1, \quad y(-1) = 1.$$

To check our result we can use the Rodriguez formula to obtain:

$$P_n(x) = \frac{1}{2^n n!}\frac{d^n}{dx^n}[(x^2-1)^n] = \left\{1, x, \frac{1}{2}(3x^2-1), \frac{1}{2}(5x^3-3x), \ldots\right\}.$$

The numerical solutions for Legendre polynomials are shown below.

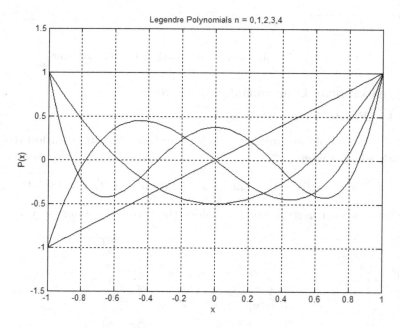

Figure 31: Legendre polynomials.

5.2.7 *Boundary Layer with Linear Differential Equation*

An example of a differential equation describing boundary layers is given by

$$\epsilon y'' - x^2 y' - y = 0, \quad y(0) = 0, \quad y(1) = 1.$$

With $\epsilon = 0.05$ and 0.005, the numerical solution is shown below.

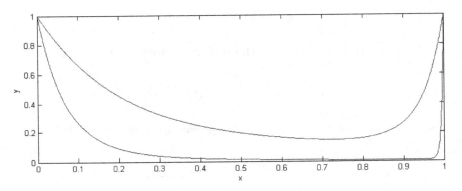

Figure 32:   Linear differential equation: Boundary Layer.

5.3 Nonlinear Differential Equations

5.3.1 *Finite Time Blow-up*

As a first example we can compute a finite time blow-up solution to the initial value problem.

$$u' = u^2, \quad u(0) = 1. \quad \text{The exact solution is: } u(t) = 1/(1 - t).$$

We used predictor-corrector to explore the problem numerically.

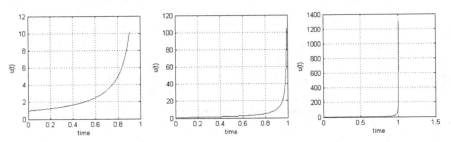

Figure 33:   Finite time blow-up.

Notice that as t approaches 1, the value of $u(t)$ diverges to infinity. We can also study a different family of solutions based on the slight modification

$$u' = 1 + u^2, \quad u(0) = 0.$$

In this case the discretization is

$$\frac{u_{i+1} - u_i}{\Delta t} = 1 + u_i^2,$$

although this may require very fine time steps to resolve solutions accurately. A numerical solution is shown using Forward Euler together with the exact solution $y = \tan(t)$.

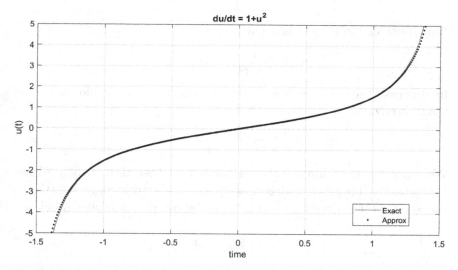

Figure 34: Finite time blow up: $u(t) = \tan(t)$. (Start the integration from $t = 0$ and integrate forward and backward in time.)

It is also of interest to consider

$$u' = 1 - u^2, \quad u(0) = 0.$$

Similarly, in this case the discretization is

$$\frac{u_{i+1} - u_i}{\Delta t} = 1 - u_i^2.$$

A numerical solution is shown using Forward Euler together with the exact solution $y = \tanh(t)$.

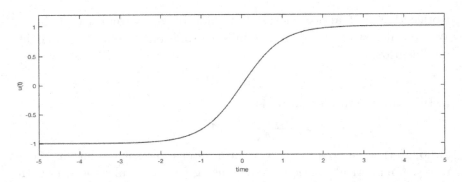

Figure 35:   Numerical and exact solution for $u(t) = \tanh(t)$.

Now consider the inverse problem

$$u' = \frac{1}{1+t^2}, \quad u(0) = 0.$$

In this case the solution is $y = a\tan(x)$ and it does not blow up. Use the discretization

$$\frac{u_{i+1} - u_i}{\Delta t} = \frac{1}{1+t_i^2}.$$

We solve this as an initial value problem, by integrating in the positive t-direction and negative t-direction separately starting from $t = 0$. Using this strategy, the entire $y = a\tan(t)$ can be computed as shown below.

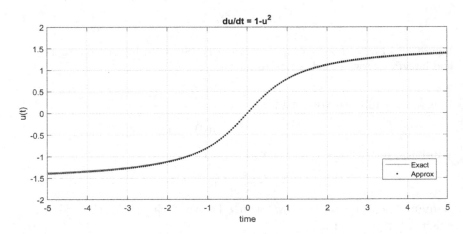

Figure 36:   Numerical and exact solution for $u(t) = a\tan(t)$.

Similarly one can also show that the inverse problem of $\tanh(t)$ has the solution $u(t) = \operatorname{atanh}(t)$, which is unbounded as shown below.

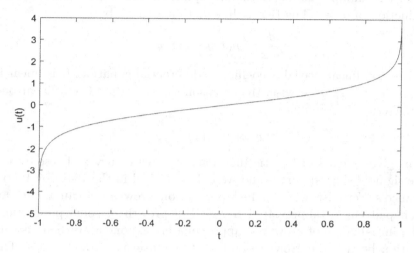

5.3.2 *Spontaneous Singularities*

The exact solution to

$$y' = y^2/(1 - xy), \quad y(0) = 1$$

is $y = \exp(xy)$ which has undefined (infinite) slope at $x = 1/e$. When solving this problem numerically, one must be careful not to compute a spurious solution by integrating through the singularity.

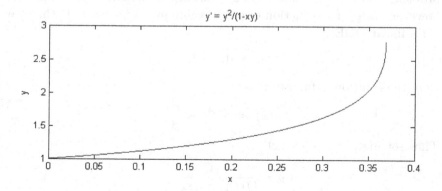

Figure 37:   Spontaneous singularities.

5.3.3 *Bernoulli Equation*

Another example is the Bernoulli equation, which can be solved by reduction of order. The Bernoulli equation is given by:

$$\frac{dy}{dx} = p(x)y - g(x)y^a.$$

It is a non-linear, variable coefficient differential equation. It is linear if $a = 0$ or $a = 1$. Otherwise, the equation can be reduced to a linear one if we set:

$$u(x) = [y(x)]^{1-a}.$$

This gives a class of logistic functions or logistic curves. These curves are sigmoid shaped curves and were first studied in the 1840s by Pierre François Verhulst who studied population growth. It can model an S-shaped curve (abbreviated S-curve) of growth of some population. The initial stage of growth is approximately exponential; then, as saturation begins, the growth slows, and at maturity, growth stops. The logistic function finds applications in a range of fields, including artificial neural networks, biology, biomathematics, demography, economics, chemistry, mathematical psychology, probability, sociology, political science, and statistics. The Verhulst equation is given by

$$\frac{dy}{dx} = Ay - By^2, \quad A > 0, \quad B > 0.$$

This equation is sometimes referred to as the logistic equation. Notice here the equation is non-linear. We seek non-trivial solutions to this problem (clearly $y = 0$ is always a solution). In general this is difficult; however, using the reduction of order technique, we set $u = \frac{1}{y}$, then we get a linear ODE:

$$u' + Au = B.$$

Here the solution is found to be

$$u(x) = ce^{-Ax} + \frac{B}{A}.$$

Thus setting $y = 1/u$ we get

$$y = \frac{1}{(B/A) + ce^{-Ax}}.$$

Examples should be solved numerically using Predictor-Corrector Scheme and plotted for the two cases: (1) $y(0) > A/B$, and (2) $y(0) < A/B$. A large range of initial values is shown.

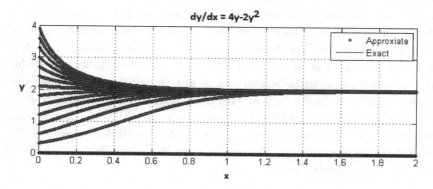

Figure 38:   Bernoulli equation.

In the case

$$\frac{dy}{dx} = Ay - By^3, \quad A > 0, \quad B > 0$$

a third steady state is possible as shown below.

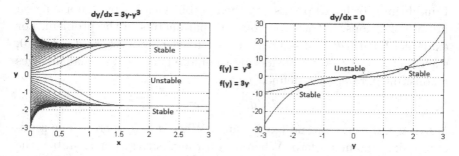

Figure 39:   Bernoulli equation: numerical integration for a range of initial values (*left*), location of the fixed points (*right*).

5.3.4   *Saddle Node Bifurcations*

A differential equation $dx/dt = f(x)$ has a solution with a certain behavior depending on the initial condition. For example, asymptotically it might be that $x(t)$ tends to 0, some other constant value, or positive or negative infinity (blow up) in the limit as t tends to infinity. Of particular interest in the study of differential equations is identifying fixed points and their stability. Equilibria, or fixed points, typically are either stable, unstable or semi-stable. The idea of a stable equilibrium is that after any small perturbation of the object, it will return to the equilibrium position, like a ball at the bottom of a valley. In contrast to this, for an unstable equilibrium, like a ball on a hilltop, after a small perturbation the object moves away from the equilibrium position. For a semi-stable equilibrium, the equilibrium behaves like it is stable on one side and unstable on the other.

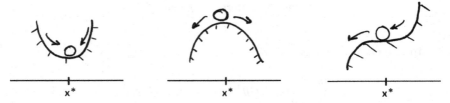

Figure 40:   (*Left*) A stable equilibrium, (*middle*) an unstable equilibrium, (*right*) a semi-stable equilibrium.

Equilibrium (or fixed) points and their stability can depend not only on initial conditions, but also on constant parameters in the problem. For example, for $dx/dt = 4 - x^2$, there are fixed points where $dx/dt = 0$, such that $x = \pm 2$. Now considering the more general case that involves a constant parameter a defined by

$$dx/dt = a - x^2.$$

When $a < 0$, there are no fixed points. When $a = 0$, there is one semi-stable fixed point at zero. When $a > 0$ the positive root is stable, the negative root is unstable. Plots of the solutions for many different initial conditions are shown below.

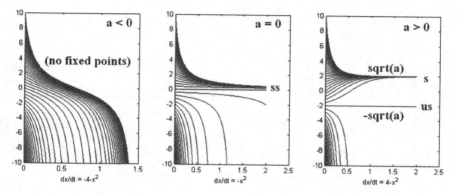

Figure 41: Representative numerical solutions for all cases in the parameter a.

There are many interesting examples involving bifurcations, but the standard archetypes are: saddle node, transcritical, and pitchfork. Pitchfork bifurcations occur in super-critical and sub-critical varieties.

5.3.5 *Transcritical Bifurcations*

In a saddle node bifurcation, a fixed point appears as the bifurcation parameter is varied. Then the equilibrium solution splits into two branches with opposite stability. In contrast to this, in a transcritical bifurcation, there are two equilibrium branches that coalesce and switch stability with each other. The standard form for a transcritical bifurcation is

$$\frac{dx}{dt} = rx - x^2.$$

Another example of this phenomenon occurs in the example

$$\frac{dx}{dt} = rx - re^x.$$

The bifurcation diagram is shown below for this example.

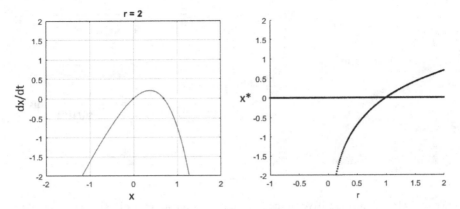

Figure 42: Transcritical bifurcation. (*Left*) Phase portrait for the specific value of $r = 2$. The fixed points, or equilibrium solutions occur where $\frac{dx}{dt} = rx - re^x = 0$. (*Right*) Bifurcation diagram showing the fixed points for every value of the bifurcation parameter in $-1 < r < 2$. The transcritical bifurcation occurs at $r = 1$.

5.3.6   *Pitchfork Bifurcations*

In the pitchfork bifurcation, one fixed point becomes three at a critical value of the bifurcation parameter. The standard form for this type of bifurcation is

$$\frac{dx}{dt} = rx - x^3.$$

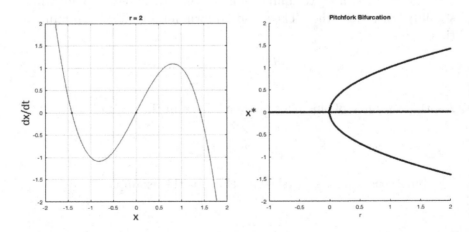

Figure 43:   Pitchfork bifurcation.

5.3.7 *Hopf Bifucations*

In a Hopf bifurcation a limit cycle emerges, which can attract (stable) or repel (unstable) orbits. A classical Hopf bifurcation is give by the equations [Strogatz]

$$\frac{dr}{dt} = ar - r^3$$

$$\frac{d\theta}{dt} = 1.$$

The discretization of the equations is given by

$$\frac{r_{n+1} - r_n}{\Delta t} = ar_n - r_n^3$$

$$\frac{\theta_{n+1} - \theta_n}{\Delta t} = 1.$$

Note there is a transformation between polar and rectangular coordinates using

$$x = r\cos(\theta), \quad \text{and} \quad y = r\sin(\theta).$$

Here are numerical solutions which show how a stable fixed point at $(r, \theta) = (x, y) = (0, 0)$ becomes an unstable fixed point and a limit cycle emerges for $(a > 0)$. To produce plots like these, fix the value of the parameter a and integrate numerically for many different initial conditions $(r(0), \theta(0))$. The points in the figure are for different initial conditions, and the lines are the trajectories that the solution will follow in time $(r(t), \theta(t))$ starting from each given initial value and computed forward in time.

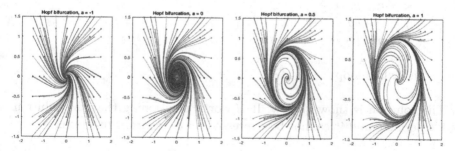

Figure 44: Hopf bifurcation: many trajectories for different initial conditions are plotted in the x-y plane, left to right for $a = -1$, $a = 0$, $a = 0.5$, and $a = 1$.

5.3.8 *Jerk Equation and Its Chaotic Solution*

Here we study a Jerk equation that admits a chaotic soution. The equation is given by a third-order equation

$$\frac{d^3y}{dt^2} + A\frac{d^2y}{dt^2} - \frac{dy}{dt}^2 + y = 0.$$

The third-order Jerk equation is one of the simplest models that admits a chaotic solution. One can see the chaotic behavior with the choice of $A = 2.017$.[3] To obtain a numerical solution re-write the third-order equation as a system of three first-order equations given by

$$\frac{dx}{dt} = v$$

$$\frac{dv}{dt} = a$$

$$\frac{da}{dt} = j = -A \cdot a + v^2 - x.$$

Follow this psuedo-code to get the solution.

Set: $x = 0.02, v = 0, a = 0, h = 0.01, A = 2.017, imax$
while $i < imax$
$x = x + h \cdot v$
$v = v + h \cdot a$
$j = -A \cdot a + v \cdot v - x$
$a = a + h \cdot j$
$i = i + 1$
end while loop

The solution is shown below. It is worth mentioning that the solution is aperiodic and it cannot be expressed by elementary functions.

---

[3] J. C. Sprott, Some simple chaotic jerk functions. *Am. J. Phys.* 65, 537–543 (1997).

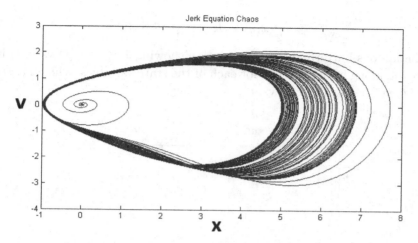

Figure 45:   Chaotic solution to third-order Jerk equation.

5.3.9   *Lorenz Equation and Its Chaotic Solution*

We use the predictor-corrector method to solve the Lorenz equations for atmospheric convection (weather modeling)

$$\frac{dx}{dt} = \sigma(y - x)$$

$$\frac{dy}{dt} = x(\rho - z) - y$$

$$\frac{dz}{dt} = xy - \beta z$$

starting from $(x(0), y(0), z(0)) = (5, 5, 5)$, up to time $t = 70$, subject to the parameter choices: $\sigma = 10, r = 28, b = 8/3$. We use the predictor-corrector method. Here first solve for the predicted values $\bar{x}, \bar{y}$ and $\bar{z}$ using the discretization for first order system

$$\frac{\bar{x} - x_i}{\Delta t} = \sigma(y_i - x_i)$$

$$\frac{\bar{y} - y_i}{\Delta t} = x_i(\rho - z_i) - y_i$$

$$\frac{\bar{z} - z_i}{\Delta t} = x_i y_i - \beta z_i.$$

Then, make the correction step

$$\frac{x_{i+1} - x_i}{\Delta t} = \frac{1}{2}(\sigma(y_i - x_i)) + \frac{1}{2}(\sigma(\bar{y} - \bar{x}))$$

$$\frac{y_{i+1} - y_i}{\Delta t} = \frac{1}{2}(x_i(\rho - z_i) - y_i) + \frac{1}{2}(\bar{x}(\rho - \bar{z}) - \bar{y})$$

$$\frac{z_{i+1} - z_i}{\Delta t} = \frac{1}{2}(x_i y_i - \beta z_i) + \frac{1}{2}(\bar{x}\bar{y} - \beta\bar{z}).$$

The famous butterfly attractor solution showing $x(t)$ vs. $y(t)$ vs. $z(t)$ is shown, along with solutions for each of the state variables, which is $x(t)$ vs. t, $y(t)$ vs. t, and $z(t)$ vs. t, respectively.

$$\frac{dx}{dt} = \sigma(y - x) \qquad \frac{dy}{dt} = x(\rho - z) - y \qquad \frac{dz}{dt} = xy - \beta z$$

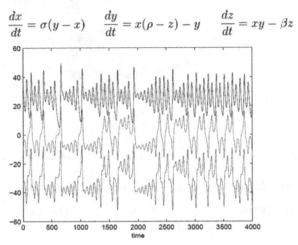

**This is the solution
to the system of equations
for x(t), y(t) and z(t)**

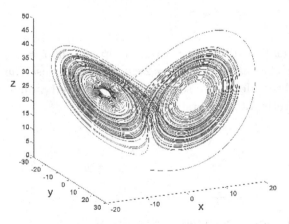

**This is called an attractor
which is just another representation
of x(t), y(t) and z(t)**

Figure 46:   Lorenz equations.

To demonstrate sensitivity to initial conditions (SIC), which is a defining property of chaos, start many initial conditions all very close to each other, then integrate the system in time. Shown here is 1,000 initial values all clustered together initially, but randomly, within a relatively small cube, and their final (x, y, z) locations after integrating for several time steps.

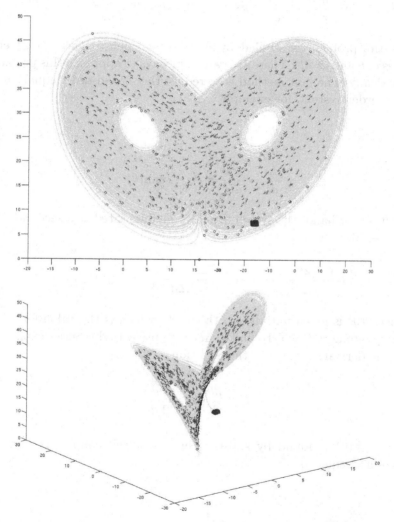

Figure 47:   Demonstrating sensitivity to initial conditions (SIC). 1,000 initial values close together are integrated numerically. The trajectories all end up on the same attractor, but in very different places!

5.3.10   Nonlinear Spring: Pendulums and the Phase Plane

The damped pendulum is a classical and standard example used in education that is good for building intuition

$$\frac{d^2\theta}{dt^2} - c\frac{d\theta}{dt} + k\sin\theta = 0, \quad k \geq 0, \quad c \geq 0.$$

First the problem is studied by plotting the phase space for several values of θ and $d\theta/dt$. There are two main ways to approach this problem numerically. The first method is to reduce the second-order equation to a first-order system, for example

$$\frac{d\theta}{dt} = u$$

$$\frac{du}{dt} = \frac{d^2\theta}{dt^2} = cu - k\sin(\theta).$$

On the other hand, the system can also be integrated as a second-order problem directly.

$$\frac{\theta_{n+1} - 2\theta_n + \theta_{n-1}}{\Delta t^2} - c\frac{\theta_{n+1} - \theta_{n-1}}{2\Delta t} + k\sin(\theta_n) = 0.$$

Notice $\theta(0)$ is given initially, so this is θ_1, which is the value for $i = 1$ corresponding to $t = 0$. To find $\theta(\Delta t) = \theta_2$ use a Taylor Series expansion and the derivative $\frac{d\theta}{dt}(0)$ in the equation

$$\theta_2 = \theta_1 + \frac{d\theta}{dt}(0) + \frac{1}{2}\frac{d^2\theta}{dt^2}(0),$$

where $\frac{d^2\theta}{dt^2}(0)$ is found by substituting the initial conditions into the differential equation.

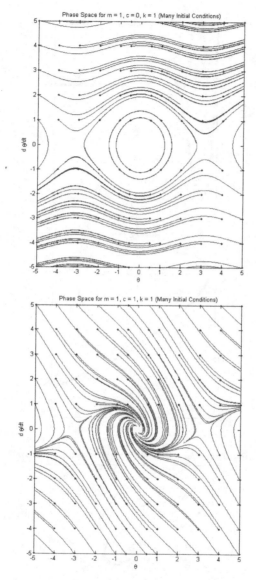

Figure 48: Damped pendulum. The dots in the plot indicate where the starting position was in the phase space.

Next the damped case is studied. Each trajectory in the phase space corresponds to a displacement solution in time. Shown here are plots of the solution, and the phase plane.

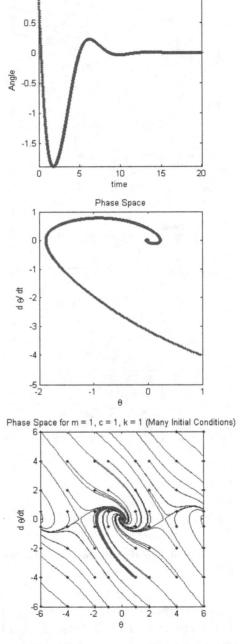

Figure 49:   Phase space for damped pendulum.

5.3.11 *Nonlinear Spring: Duffing Oscillator*

The governing equation for a Duffing Oscillator can be given by[4]

$$\frac{d^2y}{dt^2} + 2\zeta\frac{dy}{dt} + y^3 = F\cos(\Omega t).$$

A special case of this problem is the Ueda oscillator. We will study this problem numerically. The Ueda oscillator is given by

$$\frac{d^2y}{dt^2} + 2\zeta\frac{dy}{dt} + y^3 = F\cos(t).$$

Here ζ is the damping coefficient. Typical examples for different F values are shown here for $\zeta = 0.01$, $F = 0.7$ and $F = 0.1$.

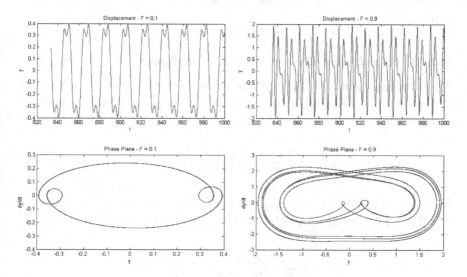

Figure 50:   Ueda oscillator.

Both state space and phase plane analysis show, for different values of F and a fixed value of ζ, how the solution behaves.

---

[4]Kovacic, I.; Brennan, M.J. *The Duffing Equation: Nonlinear Oscillators and Their Behaviour*, Wiley (2011).

5.3.12 *Nonlinear Damping: Van der Pol Oscillator*

The Van der Pol oscillator is a non-conservative oscillator with non-linear damping. It evolves in time according to the second-order differential equation:

$$\frac{d^2y}{dx^2} - k(1 - y^2)\frac{dy}{dx} + y = 0.$$

First the problem is studied by plotting the displacement and phase space for several values of the parameter k, for example $k = 0, 0.1, 20$ as shown, while fixing the initial conditions to be $y = 0.1$ and $dy/dt = 0$. Next the problem is studied by varying the initial position and velocity conditions while fixing $k = 1.5$.

These two different approaches give a sense of how complicated the solution space for a problem like this with just a single free parameter can be.

5.3.13 *Nonlinear Damping: Rayleigh Equation*

The Rayleigh oscillator (of nonlinear acoustics) is similar to the Van der Pol oscillator. It evolves in time according to the second-order differential equation:

$$\frac{d^2y}{dt^2} - \epsilon\left(\frac{dy}{dt} - \frac{1}{3}\left(\frac{dy}{dt}\right)^3\right) + y = 0.$$

Use $\epsilon = 0.2$ and the initial conditions $y(0) = 0$ and $y'(0) = 2a$ for $a = 0.05$. The asymptotic solution (Bender and Orzag), in this case is

$$y = \frac{2a\sin(t)}{\sqrt{exp(-\epsilon t) + a^2(1 - exp(-\epsilon t)))}}.$$

Unlike the Van der Pol case, now a straightforward discretization of the governing equation leads to a nonlinear equation for y_{n+1}.

$$\frac{y_{n+1} - 2y_n + y_{n-1}}{\Delta t^2} - \epsilon\left(\frac{y_{n+1} - y_{n-1}}{2\Delta t} - \frac{1}{3}\left(\frac{y_{n+1} - y_{n-1}}{2\Delta t}\right)^3\right)$$
$$+ y_n = 0.$$

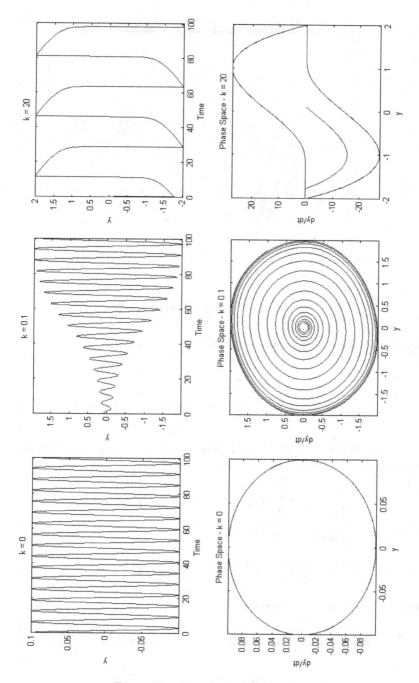

Figure 51: Van der Pol oscillator.

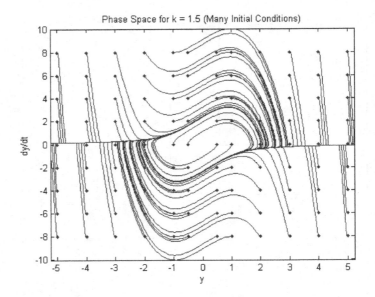

Figure 52:   Van der Pol phase space.

In order to solve this problem, define

$$y_{n-1/2} = \frac{y_n + y_{n-1}}{2}$$

$$v_{n-1/2} = \frac{y_n - y_{n-1}}{dt}.$$

First compute $v_n = \frac{dy}{dt}$ at grid point n by applying the equation in terms of v

$$\frac{v_n - v_{n-1}}{\Delta t} - \epsilon \left(v_{n-1/2} - \frac{1}{3} \left(v_{n-1/2} \right)^3 \right) + y_{n-1/2} = 0.$$

Then solve for y_{n+1} according to

$$\frac{y_{n+1} - 2y_n + y_{n-1}}{\Delta t^2} - \epsilon \left(v_n - \frac{1}{3} \left(v_n \right)^3 \right) + y_n = 0$$

and in the usual way the solver is

$$y_{n+1} = 2y_n - y_{n-1} + \Delta t^2 \left(\epsilon \left(v_n - \frac{1}{3} \left(v_n \right)^3 \right) - y_n \right).$$

To start the calculation we use second order Taylor Series Expansion to compute y_2

$$y_2 = y_1 + v_1\Delta t + (f(v_1) - y_1)\Delta t^2/2.$$

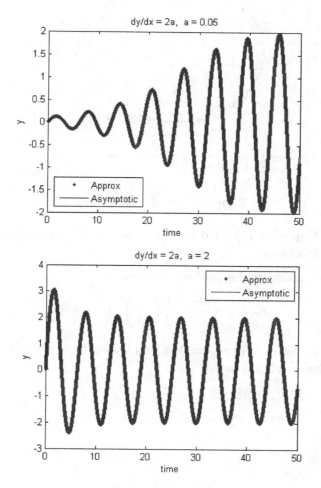

Figure 53: Rayleigh equations.

Shown here is the stable limit cycle in phase space for two values of $a = 0.05$ and $a = 2$. A very fine mesh is required for the case $a = 2$.

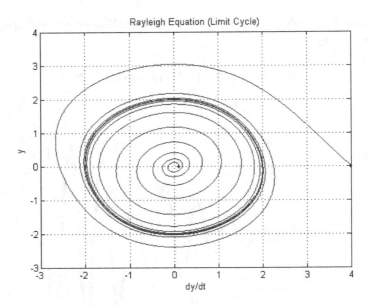

Figure 54:   Stable limit cycles.

5.3.14   *Rayleigh Equation as a Singular Perturbation Problem*

Another variation of this problem is given by

$$\epsilon \frac{d^2 y}{dt^2} - \left(\frac{dy}{dt} - \frac{1}{3} \left(\frac{dy}{dt} \right)^3 \right) + y = 0$$

for small values of ϵ. Here $\epsilon = 0.05$ and uses $y(0) = 0.9$ and $\frac{dy(0)}{dt} = 0$. The results are shown here.

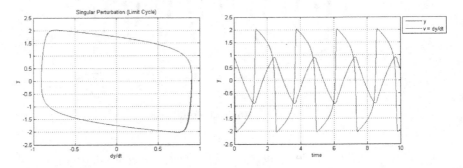

Figure 55:   Rayleigh equation as a singular perturbation problem.

5.3.15   *Nonlinear Mass: Relativistic Restoring Force*

In the case that velocity is very large it is sometimes necessary to consider the effects of relativity, leading to the relativistic oscillator equation[5]

$$\frac{d}{dt}\left(m\frac{\dot{x}}{\sqrt{1-\dot{x}^2/c^2}}\right)=-kx.$$

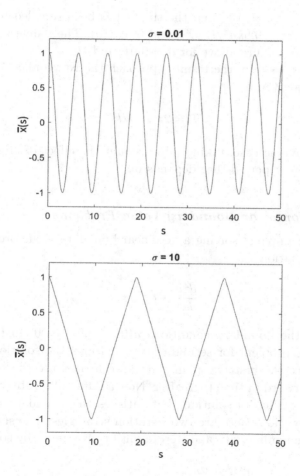

---

[5]D. Clark *et al.*, Relativistic linear restoring force, *Eur. J. Phys.*, 33–1041 (2012).

This form of the equation is equivalent to

$$m\frac{dx^2}{dt^2} = -kx(1 - \dot{x}/c^2)^{3/2}.$$

An example is solved according to the one parameter equation

$$\frac{d^2\bar{x}}{ds^2} = -\bar{x}(1 - 2\sigma v^2)^{3/2},$$

where $\bar{x} = x/a$, $v = \frac{1}{a}\frac{dx}{ds}$ and the time t has been rescaled to s, where $s = t\sqrt{k/m}$, $\sigma = 0.5ka^2/(mc^2)$, and $a = x(0)$. The numerical solution is shown in the figure above for $\sigma = 0.01$, and 10.

As σ goes to zero, the results approach the Newtonian case, where the period is given by

$$T = 2\pi\sqrt{m/k}.$$

In the relativistic case, taking into account the effect of large velocity gives a different period that depends on σ.

5.3.16 *Nonlinear Boundary Value Problems*

As a first example of solving a nonlinear boundary value problem consider the equation

$$\frac{d^2u}{dx^2} + e^{-u} = 0$$

subject to the boundary conditions $u(0) = u(1) = 0$. In the case of initial value problem for second-order equations the solution is easier because once the first two points are known, just use the equation to integrate forward in time thereafter. Now a different strategy is needed. First guess an initial solution that satisfies the boundary conditions, then use iteration. Here are two iteration strategies. The simplest way is to lag the nonlinearity and iterate until convergence by solving

$$\frac{u_{i+1}^{n+1} - 2u_i^{n+1} + u_{i-1}^{n+1}}{dx^2} + e^{-u_i^n} = 0.$$

Choosing an initial guess of $u(x) = x(x-1)$, the solution will converge in about 6 iterates to an error of less than 10^{-5}. A better method, that will converge faster, is to correct the residual as follows

$$\frac{\tilde{u}_{i+1} - 2\tilde{u}_i + \tilde{u}_{i-1}}{\Delta x^2} - \tilde{u}_i e^{-u_i^n} = -\left(\frac{u_{i+1}^n - 2u_i^n + u_{i-1}^n}{\Delta x^2} + e^{-u_i^n}\right),$$

then solve for $\tilde{u}$ and update

$$u^{n+1} = u^n + \tilde{u}.$$

This solution should converge faster. The solution is shown here.

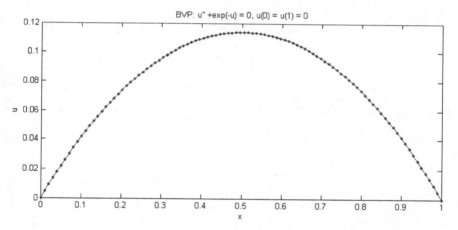

Figure 56:   Nonlinear boundary value problem.

The case of

$$\frac{d^2 u}{dx^2} + e^u = 0$$

is a more difficult problem and will be considered in the study of combustion.

PART II

Applications in Science and Engineering

The applications are divided into dynamics and vibrations, solid and structural mechanics, fluid mechanics, heat transfer, chemical reactions and combustion. In each project a problem is introduced, a governing equation is given with its discretization, and a numerical solution is shown. In all cases, we use the modules to solve the problems.

6. Dynamics and Vibrations

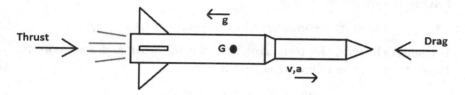

Figure 57:   Rocket science!

6.1   Rocket Dynamics in Space (Tsiolkovsky Equation)

Consider a rocket in space with no gravity and no drag. Consider two
states of the rocket at $t = 0$ and $t = \Delta t$ where the velocity changed in
magnitude, but not in direction and the mass changed with Δm due to
the loss of the fuel consumed. Consider the magnitude of the momentum
of the rocket at $t = 0$,

$$M = m \cdot v.$$

Next consider the momentum of the rocket in the same direction at
$t + \Delta t$

$$M = (m + \Delta m) \cdot (v + \Delta v).$$

The momentum of the fuel leaving the rocket is

$$\Delta m_f \cdot v_f.$$

Notice that v_f, the exhaust velocity of the fuel, is negative since it is in
the opposite direction of the velocity of the rocket. From conservation
of mass

$$m = (m + \Delta m) + \Delta m_f,$$

and

$$\Delta m = -\Delta m_f,$$

which means the mass of the rocket decreases by the amount of fuel
burned. Since there is no external force applied to the system, Newton's

second law of motion states that the magnitude of the total momentum does not change. Hence, the initial momentum should be equal to the sum of the momentum of the rocket and the momentum of the fuel leaving the rocket in time Δt, or

$$mv = [mv + m\Delta v + v\Delta m + \Delta m \Delta v] + [\Delta m_f \cdot v_f].$$

For small changes, the term $\Delta m \Delta v$ is second order and we ignore it. Hence we have the following equation

$$m\Delta v = -v\Delta m - \Delta m_f v_f,$$

or, substituting for Δm_f

$$m\Delta v = -\Delta m \cdot (v - v_f) = \Delta m \cdot v_{FR},$$

where $v_{FR} = v_f - v$ is the relative velocity of the exhaust fuel to the rocket. The Tsiolkovsky equation is

$$m\Delta v = \Delta m \cdot v_{FR}.$$

Then

$$\frac{dv}{dm} = v_{FR}\frac{1}{m}, \quad v(0) = 0,$$

and the solution is given by

$$\frac{v}{v_{FR}} = \ln(m/m_0),$$

or

$$\frac{v}{|v_{FR}|} = \ln(m_0/m).$$

Notice that v_{FR} is constant (negative). Alternatively

$$m\frac{dv}{dt} = \frac{dm}{dt} \cdot v_{FR}, \quad v(0) = 0.$$

If the rate of discharge $(dm/dt = D)$ is constant (and negative), so $D < 0$, and $m = m_0 + Dt$, then

$$m\frac{dv}{dt} = F,$$

where F is a positive constant

$$F = D \cdot v_{FR},$$

and $v(0) = 0$. Solving the above problem we can find $v = v(t)$. It is obvious from this equation that the maximum rate of discharge possible is needed, along with the maximum exhaust velocity from the exit of the nozzle. These issues will be discussed further in the sections for compressible flow in nozzles and rocket combustion.

Tsiolkovsky also introduced the idea of multistage rockets. In this case, the fuel is distributed into different tanks that can be dropped after the fuel is used up, and thereby reduces the overall mass that needs to be accelerated.

6.2   Vertical Motion of Launch Vehicle

An example of Tsiolkovsky equation with the gravity effect added is given by

$$m\frac{dv}{dt} = F - mg.$$

In this equation $F = v_{FR}\frac{dm}{dt}$, where $v_{FR} = -2000\,\text{m/s}$ is the exhaust velocity, $\frac{dm}{dt} = -100\,\text{kg/s}$ is the fuel burn rate, the gravity $g = 9.8\,\text{m/s}^2$ and m is the mass of the rocket, its fuel and payload. Let the mass of the rocket and payload be $700\,\text{kg}$, and the mass of the fuel be $4000\,\text{kg}$. Start with an initial velocity of $v(0) = 0\,\text{m/s}$. Using forward Euler Method

$$\frac{v^{n+1} - v^n}{\Delta t} = f(v^n).$$

The velocity is plotted as a function of time, and the velocity as a function of the mass ratio is also plotted, until the rocket runs out of fuel. The mass ratio is the initial mass divided by the current mass and is equal to one initially, then is increasing in time. Cases taking into account lift and drag forces can be considered as well.

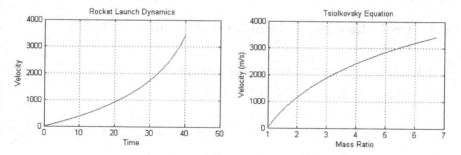

Figure 58:   Initial vertical motion of launch vehicle.

6.3 Parachute Equation with Constant Drag Coefficient

The skydiver equation of motion is governed by

$$m\frac{dv}{dt} = mg - bv^2$$

where $g = 9.8\,\text{m/s}^2$, $m \approx 72\,\text{kg}$, the mass of a person, and the acceleration is $a = \frac{dv}{dt}$. When $v_0 = v(0) = 10\,\text{m/s}$ the solution is:

$$v(t) = \sqrt{\frac{m \cdot g}{b}} \left(\frac{1 + ce^{-p \cdot t}}{1 - ce^{-p \cdot t}} \right)$$

where:

$$k = \sqrt{\frac{m \cdot g}{b}}, \quad c = \frac{v_0 - k}{v_0 + k}, \quad p = \frac{2 \cdot k \cdot b}{m}.$$

Let $b = 30$, $k = 4.87$, $p = 4.02$. A numerical solution of this equation compared with the exact solution is shown below.

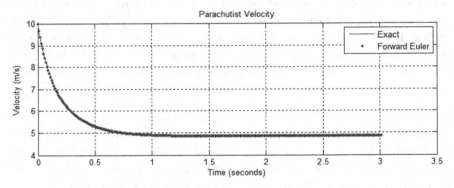

Figure 59: Parachutist equation with constant drag.

6.4 Projectiles and Orbital Mechanics of Two-Body Problem

6.4.1 *Cannon Fire Over a Flat Surface*

In this example the equations of motion are:

$$\frac{dx}{dt} = u, \quad m\frac{du}{dt} = 0$$

$$\frac{dy}{dt} = v, \quad m\frac{dv}{dt} = -mg,$$

where: $g = 9.8\,\text{m/s}^2$ the gravitational constant, u is the velocity in the x-direction, v is the velocity in the y-direction. Initially, there is a launch velocity V that is decomposed into initial u_0 and v_0 components:

$$u_0 = |V|\cos(\theta), \quad v_0 = |V|\sin(\theta),$$

where the launch angle is θ and the initial speed $|V|$. The point of launch is at the origin of coordinates, so $(x(0), y(0)) = (0,0)$. In this case the equations can be written as two second order equations

$$\frac{d^2 x}{dt^2} = 0$$

$$\frac{d^2 y}{dt^2} = -g.$$

Notice the equations are decoupled and so they can be solved independently. Together with the initial conditions plots of trajectories are shown below by using $\Delta t = 1/100, |V| = 10, 0 < \theta < \pi/2$. The height is plotted as a function of distance in the $x - y$ plane.

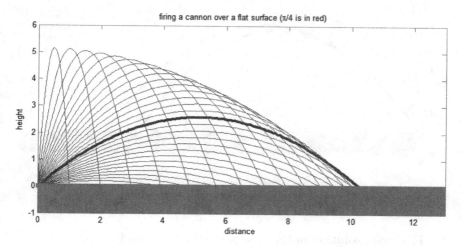

Figure 60: Projectile motion.

6.4.2   *Cannon Fire with Linear Drag*

To include air resistance the equations of motion are:

$$\frac{d^2x}{dt^2} = -k\frac{dx}{dt}$$

$$\frac{d^2y}{dt^2} = -g - k\frac{dy}{dt}$$

where: $g = 9.8\,\text{m/s}^2$ the gravitational constant, u is the velocity in the x-direction, v is the velocity in the y-direction. Again, initially we set the velocity decomposed into u and v components:

$$u_0 = |V|\cos(\theta), \quad |V| = v_0\sin(\theta),$$

where θ is the initial launch angle. The point of launch is at the origin of coordinates, so $(x(0), y(0)) = (0, 0)$. Together with the initial conditions, we plot trajectories use $\Delta t = 1/100, |V| = 10, \theta_0 = \pi/4$. We plot the height as a function of distance in the $x - y$ plane for the zero drag case, and a case with $k = 0.12$ for a drag force proportional to low speed air resistance.

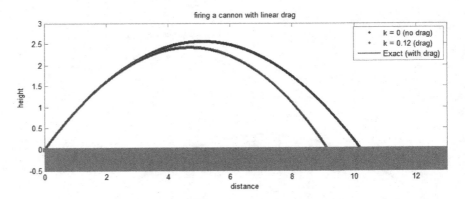

Figure 61:   Cannon fire with linear drag.

The exact solution in the case with drag is given by

$$x_{\text{exact}} = v_0/k(1 - \exp(-kt))\cos(\theta_0)$$

$$y_{\text{exact}} = v_0/k(1 - \exp(-kt))\sin(\theta_0) + g/k^2(1 - kt - \exp(-kt)).$$

 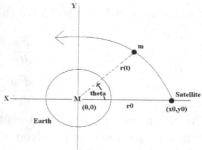

Figure 62: Earth and a satellite.

6.4.3 *Two-Body Problem: Earth and a Satellite*

The force of Newtonian gravitation in the two-body orbital system is given by:

$$F = -\frac{mMG}{r^2}.$$

The force decomposed into x-y components is given by:

$$F_x = -\frac{mMG}{r^2}\cos(\theta)$$

$$F_y = -\frac{mMG}{r^2}\sin(\theta).$$

Notice that $x/r = \cos(\theta), y/r = \sin(\theta)$. Thus from Newton's law we have:

$$m\frac{d^2x}{dt^2} = F_x = -\frac{mMG}{r^2}\cos(\theta) = -x\frac{mMG}{r^{\frac{3}{2}}}$$

$$m\frac{d^2y}{dt^2} = F_y = -\frac{mMG}{r^2}\sin(\theta) = -y\frac{mMG}{r^{\frac{3}{2}}}.$$

Setting $\omega = \frac{MG}{r^{\frac{3}{2}}}$ we then have the system:

$$\frac{d^2x}{dt^2} + \omega^2 x = 0$$

$$\frac{d^2y}{dt^2} + \omega^2 y = 0.$$

We use a coordinate system centered at the center of the Earth. The following parameters are given

$t_0 = 0; \quad M = 5.9742 \times 10^{24} \, \text{kg}; \quad G = 6.67300 \times 10^{-11} \, \text{N}(\text{m/kg})^2; \quad \theta_0 = 0.$

To get the right scaling in time, choose

$$\Delta t = t_c/100; \quad t_c = r_0/v_c; \quad v_c = \sqrt{MG/r_0}.$$

Now for r_0, the initial height we will start the satellite to be launched at $h_S = 500 \times 1000$ meters above the Earth's surface. The radius of the Earth is approximately $r_E = 6378.1 \times 1000$ meters. Hence

$$r_0 = \sqrt{x_0^2 + y_0^2} = \sqrt{((r_E + h_S)\cos(\theta))^2 + 0^2}.$$

Experiment with various initial values:

$$v_0 = 0.9v_c, \quad v_0 = v_c, \quad v_0 = \sqrt{2}v_c, \quad v_0 = 1.1v_c, \quad v_0 = 1.021\sqrt{2}v_c.$$

For the second time step use the first order Taylor Series approximation (it is better of course to use second-order approximation):

$$x_1 = x_0, y_1 = v_0\Delta t, \quad r_1 = \sqrt{x_1^2 + y_1^2}, \quad w_1^2 = MG/r_1^3.$$

Then from the third time step on, use the general scheme to update x_{i+1}, y_{i+1}:

$$\frac{x_{i+1} - 2x_i + x_{i-1}}{\Delta t^2} + \omega_i^2 x_i = 0$$

$$\frac{y_{i+1} - 2y_i + y_{i-1}}{\Delta t^2} + \omega_i^2 y_i = 0$$

$$r_i = \sqrt{x_i^2 + y_i^2}$$

$$\omega_i^2 = MG/r_i^3.$$

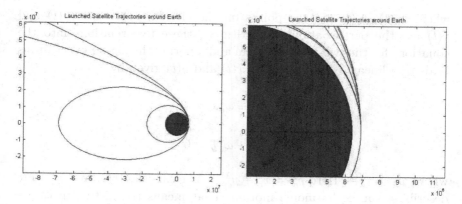

Figure 63:   Newton's cannon and satellites.

These solutions can be understood in terms of intersections of a plane with a cone, to produce: circles, ellipses, parabolas and hyperbolas.

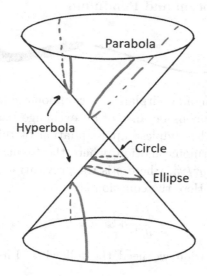

6.5   Stability of Orbits

Let us disturb a circular orbit with a small perturbation. Let's assume

$$x(t) = x_c(t) + \tilde{x}(t), \quad y(t) = y_c(t) + \tilde{y}(t)$$

where $x_c(t)$, $y_c(t)$ are the points on the circular orbit, and $\tilde{x}(t)$ and $\tilde{y}(t)$ are the perturbations. Substituting these two relations into the equations for the two-body problem and ignoring the higher order terms leads to a linearized equation for $\tilde{x}(t)$ and $\tilde{y}(t)$ given by

$$\frac{d^2\delta x}{dt^2} + \omega_c^2 \tilde{x} = 0$$

$$\frac{d^2\delta y}{dt^2} + \omega_c^2 \tilde{y} = 0$$

where $\omega_c^2 = \frac{MG}{r_c^3}$. Here $r_c^2 = x_c^2 + y_c^2$. It is clear that $\tilde{x}(t)$ and $\tilde{y}(t)$ are describing simple harmonic motion. That means the disturbances are bounded and will not grow, but at the same time they will not die out because there is no damping. Hence circular orbits are neutrally stable.

6.6   Phugoid Motion and Pendulum

The phugoid motion of an airplane is a common oscillation experienced during flight. It happens because of an exchange between kinetic and potential energy. The simplest approximation of this phenomenon is given by simple harmonic motion, where the frequency ω is given by the relation $\omega^2 = 2g^2/v_0^2$, where g is the gravitational constant and v_0 is the initial speed. Here the equation is

$$\frac{d^2h}{dt^2} + \omega^2 h = 0.$$

To derive this equation we need the following. First, the lift of the aircraft is given by

$$L = \frac{1}{2}\rho V^2 C_L S,$$

where ρ is the air density, V is the velocity of the airplane, C_L is the lift coefficient which is proportional to the angle of attack and S is a reference area. In this case, the variation of angle of attack is ignored, and hence lift is proportional to V^2. Next, the second law of motion in the vertical direction is approximated by

$$m\frac{d^2h}{dt^2} = L - mg.$$

where $L = cV^2$, and c is a constant which can be evaluated from the equilibrium conditions at $h = 0$. To evaluate the constant c, the law of conservation of potential energy plus kinetic energy is used, namely,

$$\frac{1}{2}mV^2 + mgh = \frac{1}{2}mv_0^2.$$

Hence

$$V^2 = v_0^2 - 2gh.$$

Now, substituting this relation for the lift expression above gives

$$m\frac{d^2h}{dt^2} = c(v_0^2 - 2gh) - mg.$$

Notice that c can be evaluated from the equilibrium condition where lift equals weight, or

$$cv_0^2 = mg.$$

Therefore, $c = mg/v_0^2$, hence the governing equation is

$$\frac{d^2h}{dt^2} = -\frac{2g^2}{v_0^2}h.$$

In the above analysis we ignored the drag due to friction. Moreover, adding nonlinear effects leads to more complicated equations which will not be considered here.

The problem is similar to the perturbation of a pendulum where

$$\frac{d^2\theta}{dt^2} + \omega^2\theta = 0.$$

Here $\omega^2 = g/l$. The solution is a simple harmonic motion.

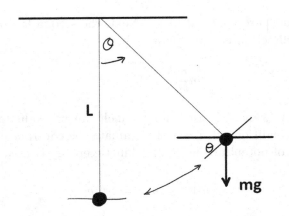

To derive the above equation, notice that the velocity tangent to the trajectory equals

$$L\frac{d\theta}{dt}$$

and the acceleration is

$$L\frac{d^2\theta}{dt^2},$$

where L is the length of the pendulum. Applying the second law of motion gives

$$Lm\frac{d^2\theta}{dt^2} = -mg\sin(\theta).$$

For small disturbances, we approximate $\sin(\theta) \approx \theta$. Gravity plays the role of a restoring force in this example. It can be shown that the total scaled energy, E, is constant

$$E = \frac{1}{2}\left(\frac{d\theta}{dt}\right)^2 + \frac{1}{2}\omega^2\theta^2.$$

Simply differentiate E with respect to time, then

$$\frac{dE}{dt} = \left(\frac{d^2\theta}{dt^2} + \omega^2\theta\right)\frac{d\theta}{dt} = 0.$$

Notice, the potential energy per unit mass is given by $g(L-L\cdot\cos(\theta))$ and the cosine function is approximated by the first three terms of Taylor series expansion, for small perturbations around the vertical line.

6.7   Why Airplanes Have Tails?

It should be mentioned that airplanes have tails to ensure static stability. The concept of static stability is simply explained in terms of the equilibrium conditions.

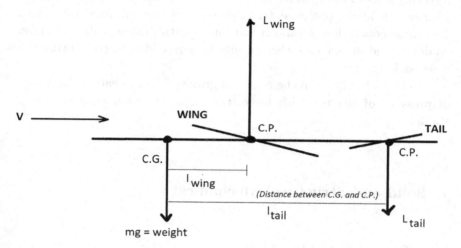

Figure 64:   C.G. is the center of gravity. C.P. is the center of pressure where the lift acts.

Instead of considering the airplane moving with velocity V in standstill air, fix the airplane and blow the air with velocity V over it, since what counts is the relative velocity (magnitude and direction). The same concept is used in wind tunnels. Notice in the sketch the angle of attack of the wing is positive, while the angle of attack of the tail is negative (the angle of attack is the relative angle between the velocity vector and the chord of the wing or tail). Hence the lift of the wing is upward and the lift of the tail is downward. For equilibrium, the total forces in the vertical direction must balance

$$L_{\text{Wing}} - L_{\text{Tail}} = W$$

where W is the weight. Also the total moment around the center of gravity (C.G.) must vanish. So,

$$l_W L_{\text{Wing}} = l_T L_{\text{Tail}}.$$

Now consider a small perturbation such that the nose of the airplanes goes up, for example due to a gust, which will lead to an increase in the angle of attack of the wing, and a decrease in the angle of attack of the tail. Therefore, the lift of the wing will be increased, and the lift of the tail will be decreased, accordingly, and the new net moment will put the nose back down. This scenario is an example of a natural restoring force. The equilibrium is stable, due to the fact that the center of gravity is ahead of the center of pressure of the combined lift forces. The same conclusion is valid if the small perturbation makes the nose go down, and in this case there would be a restoring force to bring the nose back up.

On the other hand, if the center of gravity is not ahead of the center of pressure of the total lift force, the airplane will not be statically stable.

7. Solid and Structural Mechanics

7.1 Tension in Cable

Here we study the governing equations for a cable under tension due to a weight. This kind of problem occurs in many examples, like suspension bridges.

Figure 65: Suspension bridges.

Consider a small segment of width Δx, along the cable of the form $u(x)$. At each end of a small segment along the cable, there are tensions T_1 and T_2, with horizontal components $H_1 = H_2 = H$, as shown in the figure below.

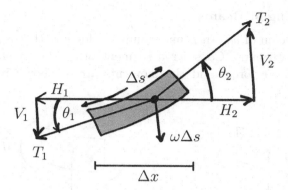

Balancing the forces in the vertical direction, where ω is the weight of the cable per unit length, then

$$v_2 = v_1 + \omega\Delta s,$$

where v_1 and v_2 are the respective vertical components of the tension force. So it follows that

$$\frac{v_2 - v_1}{H\Delta x} = \frac{\omega}{H} \Rightarrow \frac{d^2u}{dx^2} = \frac{\omega}{H}.$$

Here we used the relations

$$\frac{v_2}{H_2} = \tan(\theta_2) = \left(\frac{du}{dx}\right)_2, \quad \frac{v_1}{H_1} = \tan(\theta_1) = \left(\frac{du}{dx}\right)_1$$

and the approximation that $\Delta s \approx \Delta x$. Tension in a cable can then be approximated by the following standard boundary value problem

$$u'' = 1, \quad u(0) = 0, \quad u(1) = 0.$$

We can solve this boundary value problem using 3, 4, and 5 grid points by Gaussian elimination. Since this is a tridiagonal linear system, we use the Thomas algorithm for more points (see the Appendix).

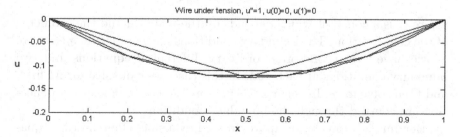

Figure 66: Tension in cable.

7.2   Bending of Beams

Consider a beam of length L under uniform loading that is simply supported at both ends. Consider a segment of the beam of width Δx, where the shear forces and the moments are as shown in the below figure.

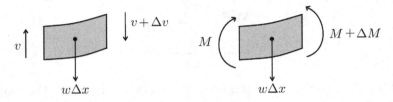

Balancing the forces in the vertical direction gives

$$\Delta v = -w\Delta x, \quad \text{or,} \quad \frac{\Delta v}{\Delta x} = -w$$

where w is the load per unit width. Balancing the moments then gives

$$\Delta M = v \cdot \Delta x - \omega\frac{\Delta x^2}{2}, \quad \text{or,} \quad \frac{\Delta M}{\Delta x} \approx v.$$

Combining these two equations gives

$$\frac{d^2 M}{dx^2} = -w,$$

with the boundary conditions $M(0) = M(L) = 0$. To find the deflection y, we use the fact that the moment is proportional to the curvature $(1/R)$, hence

$$M = C/R \approx C\frac{d^2 y}{dx^2},$$

where C is a constant which depends on the material and the geometry of the cross-section. The boundary conditions for y are $y(0) = y(L) = 0$. So we have two second-order ordinary differential equations and two boundary conditions at each end. In this case, we can solve for M first, and then solve for y. In general the two problems of moment and deflection are coupled through the boundary conditions.

Bending a beam can be approximated by a single fourth-order equation by combining the two second-order equations. In this case, the following boundary value problem is obtained

$$\frac{d^4y}{dx^4} = 1, \quad y(0) = 0, \quad y(1) = 0, \quad y_{xx}(0) = 0, \quad y_{xx}(1) = 0,$$

where $C = 1$ and $w = -1$. The exact solution is obtained by integrating four times to get

$$y_{exact} = \frac{1}{24}x^4 - \frac{1}{12}x^3 + \frac{1}{24}x^2 + 1.$$

Using the finite difference approximation for the second-order equations, the numerical solution is shown below together with the exact solution.

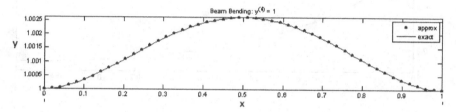

Figure 67:   Bending of beams.

7.3   Torsion of Shafts

Consider a shaft of circular cross section under torsion, with torque T at the free end and with the other end fixed at the wall. It is assumed that the torque is proportional to the twist angle θ, namely that $T = c \cdot \theta$ where c depends on the material properties of the shaft and its cross section geometry. For noncircular cross section this equation must be modified to include a term due to the bending. Hence, we have

$$-c_0 \frac{d^2\theta}{dx^2} + c\theta = T,$$

where c_0 is another constant that depends also on the material and the geometry. The boundary conditions in this case are $\theta(0) = 0$ and $\frac{d\theta}{dx}(L) = 0$, where L is the length of the shaft. The solution of this nonhomogeneous linear constant coefficient boundary value problem can be obtained analytically in terms of hyperbolic functions, where c, c_0 are positive numbers. In the following, we produce a numerical solution using a uniform grid, central difference scheme, and tridiagonal solver of the discrete algebraic equations. See the Appendix for details of the tridiagonal solver. Notice that we need a fictitious point to implement the derivative boundary condition at $x = L$. The details of the use of fictitious points are included in module 3. Torsion of a shaft can be approximated by the following boundary value problem

$$\epsilon u'' - u = 1, \quad u(0) = 0, \quad u_x(1) = 0.$$

Set $\epsilon = 0.1$ and solve this BVP for a bream of length 1.

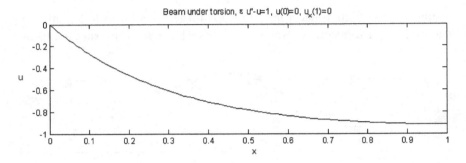

7.4   Buckling of Columns

In contrast to the bending of a beam with lateral load, in the buckling problem the load is in the axial direction as shown below for a column of length L under compressive load F.

The governing equation for the deformation $u(x)$ is derived from the fact that moment is proportional to curvature, so

$$-F \cdot u = C \frac{d^2 u}{dx^2},$$

where C is a constant which depends on the material and the geometry of the cross-section of the column, with the boundary conditions $u(0) = u(L) = 0$ (notice the sign of the moment generated by the compressive load is negative). The standard form of this problem is given by

$$u'' + \lambda u = 0, \quad u(0) = 0, \quad u(1) = 0,$$

which is an eigenvalue problem. There is a trivial solution $u = 0$, but this is not the required solution. The numerical solution of the column

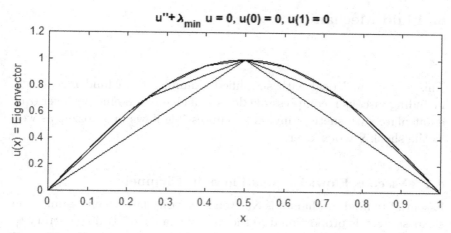

Figure 68: Showing the 3 points, 5 points, 10 points and 80 points solutions. The exact solution is $u(x) = \sin(\pi x)$.

shape is shown here for 3, 5 and many grid points, along with the exact solution, which is sinusoidal.

In order to compute the shape, it is necessary to solve for the eigenvalue. To numerically approximate the minimum eigenvalue use the method of module 4. The exact solution is $\pi^2 \approx 9.869604401$. Similarly, approximate the eigenfunction, in this case which is u(x), to get the shape of the column. Shown below are the approximations of the eigenvalue as the number of grid points increases.

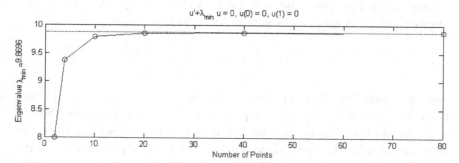

Figure 69: Approximating the eigenvalue as a function of the number of grid points compared to the exact value of π^2.

8. Fluid Mechanics

This section will deal with simplified examples from fluid mechanics, including viscous incompressible flows in a channel, boundary layer over a flat plate with suction, inviscid compressible flows in a nozzle, as well as the shock viscous layer.

8.1　Viscous Flow: Viscous Flows in Channel

Essential to fluid mechanics is Newton's viscosity law which assumes the shear stress τ is proportional to the rate of change of strain, contrary to Hooke's Law for solids which assumes the shear stress is proportional to the strain itself. Newton's viscosity law is given by

$$\tau = \mu \frac{du}{dy},$$

where μ is the viscosity coefficient. An important parameter for viscous flow in a channel is Reynold's number, Re. The Reynolds number is defined here as

$$Re = \frac{p}{\tau},$$

where p is the pressure and τ is the shear stress. Assuming the pressure is proportional to ρu^2, and τ is proportional to $\mu \frac{du}{dy}$ then Reynold's number can be defined as (assuming that $\partial u/\partial h \sim u/h$)

$$Re = \frac{\rho u h}{\mu} \quad \left(\text{or, } Re = \frac{\rho u L}{\mu} \cdot \frac{h}{L} \right).$$

Next a steady flow between parallel plates is studied. In this example, there are cases where the upper plate is moving and the lower plate is fixed. Both plates can be moving, but if their velocities are not the same then we consider the lower plate fixed and the upper plate moving with the relative velocity between the two. Of particular interest will be the velocity profile of the solution, where L is the length of the channel, p is the pressure and u is the velocity. Balancing the pressure force on a small element of fluid with the friction, and assuming u is a function of

y only, the governing equation is given by

$$\text{constant} = c = p_x = \frac{p_2 - p_1}{L} = \frac{1}{Re} u_{yy}.$$

Here the discete equation is given by

$$Re \cdot c = \frac{u_{i+1} - 2u_i + u_{i-1}}{\Delta y^2}.$$

This is a boundary value problem that needs 5 input values: the upstream pressure (p_1), the downstream pressure (p_2), the velocity of the lower plate u_{lower}, the velocity of the upper plate (u_{upper}), and the length of the channel (L). Define the constant $c = p_x$ as above. Consider 4 cases of boundary conditions to solve this problem.

$$p_2 = p_1, \quad u_{upper} = 1, \quad u_{lower} = 0$$

$$p_2 < p_1, \quad u_{upper} = 1, \quad u_{lower} = 0$$

$$p_2 > p_1, \quad u_{upper} = 1, \quad u_{lower} = 0.$$

The viscous drag, D, can be calculated via integration of the shear stress, τ, at the two walls, and it is given by

$$D = \int_0^L \tau_{lower} \, dx + \int_0^L \tau_{upper} \, dx.$$

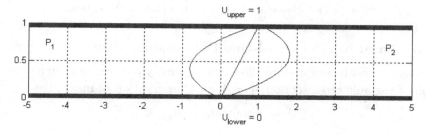

Figure 70: Channel flow.

8.2   Viscous Flow: Boundary Layer Over Flat Plate with Suction

Here the governing equation for the velocity component u, which is independent of x away from the leading edge is

$$v_0/U_\infty = 0.2 \tag{1}$$

$$-v_0 u_y = \frac{1}{\text{Re}} u_{yy}, \tag{2}$$

where Re is Reynolds number. Together with the velocity boundary conditions on the plate and in the far field.

$$u(0) = 0, \quad u(\infty) = U_\infty = 1.$$

This is a BVP. Set up the coefficient matrix of the discretized equation and boundary conditions using 8 grid points and solve the problem by Gaussian elimination.

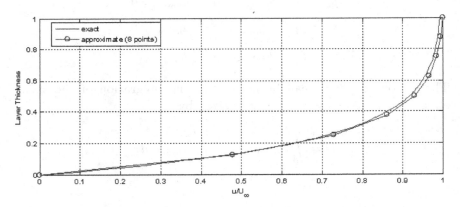

Figure 71:   Boundary layer over flat plate with suction.

8.3   Laval Nozzle: Quasi-One-Dimensional Flow

Consider first incompressible flow where density ρ is constant, in a channel of variable cross section $A = A(x)$. Conservation of mass gives:

$$A\rho u = \text{constant} = A_r \rho_r u_r.$$

Since ρ is constant,

$$\frac{u(x)}{u_r} = \frac{A_r}{A(x)}.$$

From Bernoulli's law,

$$\frac{p}{\rho} + \frac{1}{2}u^2 = \frac{p_r}{\rho} + \frac{1}{2}u_r^2,$$

and hence

$$\frac{p - p_r}{\frac{1}{2}\rho u_r^2} = 1 - \left(\frac{A_r}{A(x)}\right)^2.$$

On the other hand, to study compressible flow where density changes the situation is more complicated. Assuming conservation of mass, momentum, energy, and perfect gas law ($P = \rho RT$ where R is the gas constant), the governing equations are

$$A\rho u = w = \text{constant}$$

$$(A\rho u^2 + Ap)_x = A_x p$$

$$H = \frac{\gamma}{\gamma - 1}\frac{p}{\rho} + \frac{u^2}{2} = \text{constant}.$$

Here γ is the ratio of specific heats, and for air $\gamma = 1.4$. For smooth gradual (reversible) process which is also adiabatic, the conservation of momentum can be replaced by the relation (Poisson Adiabat)

$$\frac{p}{p_r} = \left(\frac{\rho}{\rho_r}\right)^\gamma.$$

For given $A = A(x)$, the above three equations can be solved for the unknowns: u, ρ, p using Newton's method. Let's introduce the non-dimensional version of these equations in terms of

$$\bar{u} = \frac{u}{u_r}, \quad \bar{\rho} = \frac{\rho}{\rho_r}, \quad \bar{A} = \frac{A}{A_r}, \quad \bar{p} = \frac{p}{\rho_r u_r^2}.$$

Hence,

$$\bar{A}\bar{\rho}\bar{u} = 1$$

$$\bar{p} = \frac{p}{\gamma M_r^2}$$

$$\frac{\gamma}{\gamma - 1}\frac{\bar{p}}{\bar{\rho}} + \frac{\bar{u}^2}{2} = \frac{1}{\gamma - 1}\frac{1}{M_r^2} + \frac{1}{2}$$

where the Mach number M is defined as

$$M = \frac{u}{a},$$

and a is the speed of sound. Laplace derived an equation for the speed of sound given by

$$a^2 = \frac{dp}{d\rho} = \frac{\gamma p}{\rho} = \gamma RT,$$

assuming the flow is adiabatic, meaning no heat transfer, and the process is gradual and smooth. In the above $M_r = u_r/a_r$ is a reference Mach number (at the throat).

Assuming the throat at sonic condition and choosing $A_r = A_{\text{throat}}$ and $M_r^2 = 1$, the energy equation can be reduced to a nonlinear equation for $\bar{\rho}$ only. For given $A = A(x)$, this equation can be solved by Newton's method. Hence $\bar{p}$ and $\bar{u}$ can be easily found. The smooth solution is shown in the figure below.

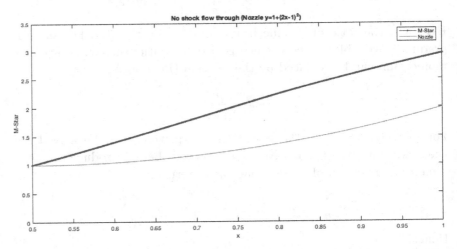

Figure 72: Smooth solution in Laval Nozzle (M-star is the same as $\bar{u}$ in the figure).

At off design conditions, a shock will appear and entropy will jump, increasing across the shock. The shock location will depend on the exit conditions, and the details are beyond the scope of this book. For more details, see [White].

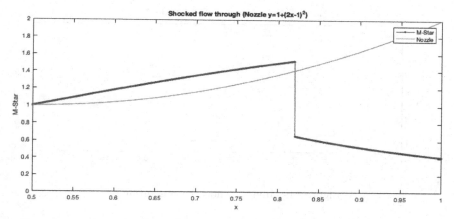

Figure 73: Shock solution in Laval Nozzle (M-star is the same as $\bar{u}$ in the figure).

8.4 Shock Viscous Layer

The shock is a thin layer of large gradient and can be considered as a discontinuous solution with a jump in density, velocity and pressure (ρ, u, p). The governing equation is given by conservation of momentum

$$\rho u u_x = -p_x + (\mu u_x)_x.$$

A simple mathematical model with similar behavior is given by

$$u u_x = \nu u_{xx}$$

with boundary conditions of u given at both ends of the domain $-1 \leq x \leq 1$:

$$u(-1) = 1, \quad u(1) = -1.$$

Central differences can be used to approximate first and second derivative terms on a uniform grid, and the resulting algebraic equations can be solved by Thomas algorithm for tridiagonal equations lagging the coefficients of the nonlinear term. A converged solution is obtained in a few iterations starting with the discontinuous solution as the initial condition.

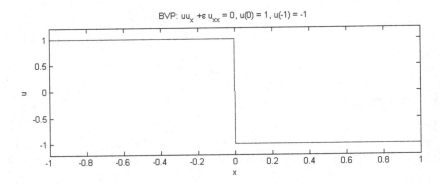

Figure 74:   Inviscid shock layer solution.

The viscous solution is shown in the figure below for different viscosity coefficients.

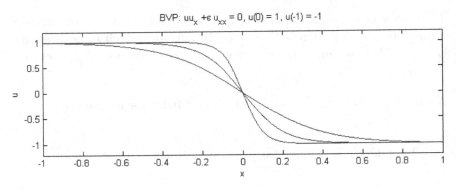

Figure 75:   Viscous shock layer solution with different viscosity coefficients.

9. Heat Transfer

In this section the model problems deal with thermal energy. All modes of heat transfer are considered, including: conduction, convection, radiation, and some combined processes.

9.1   Heat Transfer: Newton's Law of Cooling

Newton's law of cooling is very simple to understand. The environment has an ambient temperature T_∞. An object with initial temperature $T(0) = T_0$ is placed in this environment. In time the temperature of the object, $T(t)$, will approach the environmental temperature T_∞. There is a constant h that is material dependent. The key feature of this model is that the rate of change of temperature is proportional to the difference between the temperature of the object and the environmental temperature, which turns out to be a reasonable approximation for heating and cooling processes dominated by convection. An initial value problem describing convective cooling is given by

$$\frac{dT}{dt} = h(T_\infty - T), \quad T_\infty = 1, \quad T(0) = 10.$$

We used the discretization

$$\frac{T_{i+1} - T_i}{\Delta t} = h(T_\infty - T_i).$$

We plot the solution together with the steady state environmental temperature, and the result is shown below.

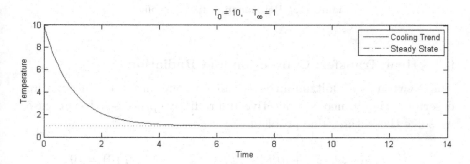

Figure 76:   Newton cooling.

Note that the temperature of the object approaches the environmental temperature asymptotically.

9.2   Heat Transfer: Stefan-Boltzmann Law of Radiation

This is an example of a nonlinear differential equation that occurs in radiation heat transfer. To model this effect, we solve the initial value problem

$$\frac{dT}{dt} = \sigma(T_\infty^4 - T^4), \quad T_\infty = 1, \quad T(0) = 10.$$

We used the discretization

$$\frac{T_{i+1} - T_i}{\Delta t} = \sigma(T_\infty^4 - T_i^4).$$

A plot of the solution together with the steady state temperature is shown below.

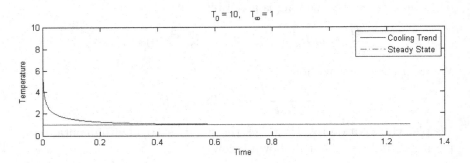

Figure 77:   Boltzmann radiative cooling.

9.3   Heat Transfer: Convection and Radiation

The Newton and Boltzmann laws can be combined into an equation describing simultaneous convective and radiative processes. In this case, we solve the initial value problem

$$\frac{dT}{dt} = h(T_\infty - T) + \sigma(T_\infty^4 - T^4), \quad T_\infty = 1, \quad T(0) = 10.$$

9.4   Heat Transfer: Heat Conduction with Heat Source

Conduction is a transfer of thermal energy within a body by direct contact with another part of the body at different temperature. The change in temperature that happens within a body is modeled by a diffusive process. The steady state temperature distribution that will result from an object of a given temperature being placed between two constant temperatures can be modeled as a boundary value problem

$$K\frac{d^2T}{dx^2} + C = 0, \quad T_{\text{left}} = 1, \quad T_{\text{right}} = 2,$$

where $K = 1$ is related to the heat conductivity, and $C = 2$ is the heat flux added to the system. In this case, we assume the object is approximated like one-dimensional rod and use N-grid points $(i = 1, \dots, N)$ along the rod. The boundary values as $T_1 = T_{\text{left}}$ and $T_N = T_{\text{right}}$, are at the rod ends. For the interior values $i = 2, \dots, N-1$ use

$$\frac{T_{i+1} - 2T_i + T_{i-1}}{\Delta x^2} + C = 0.$$

This setup will result in a system of N-coupled equations. The exact solution is found by integrating twice to get

$$T = \frac{C}{2K}x^2 + c_1 x + c_2,$$

where the boundary conditions are used to solve for the constants of integration c_1 and c_2. Here we use the numerical methods of Module 3 to plot the solution as shown below.

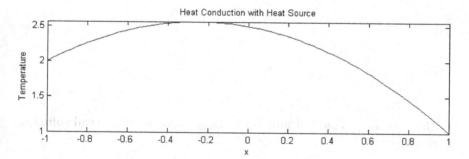

Figure 78:   Heat conduction with heat source.

9.5   Heat Transfer: Heat Conduction Through Thin Fin

In some important examples, such as turbine blades (or fins), convection and conduction processes are combined. In this case, for example, the air could be either heating or cooling by convection, while the conduction process explains the spread of the temperature difference between the fin and the air through the body of the fin. The model is given by a boundary value problem

$$K\frac{d^2T}{dx^2} - hT = 0, \quad T_{\text{left}} = T_{air} = 4, \quad T_{\text{right}} = T_{fin} = 0,$$

where K is a constant related to the conduction and h is a constant related to the convection. Assume there are N-grid points modeling the distribution of temperature along the fin ($i = 1, \ldots, N$), set the boundary values as $T_1 = T_{\text{left}}$ and $T_N = T_{\text{right}}$. For the interior values at $i = 2, \ldots, N - 1$ use

$$K\frac{T_{i+1} - 2T_i + T_{i-1}}{\Delta x^2} - hT_i = 0.$$

Here take $K = 1$, $h = 1$, $T_1 = T_{\text{left}} = 4$ and $T_N = T_{\text{right}} = 0$. The exact solution is given by

$$T = c_1 e^{\sqrt{h}x} + c_2 e^{-\sqrt{h}x},$$

for constants c_1 and c_2 that satisfy the boundary conditions. The numerical solution is shown below.

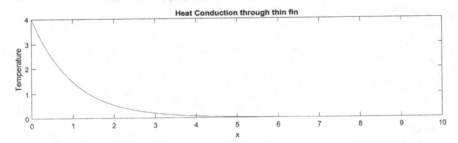

In the case $T_1 = T_{\text{left}} = 4$ and $T_N = T_{\text{right}} = 1$, the numerical solution is given by

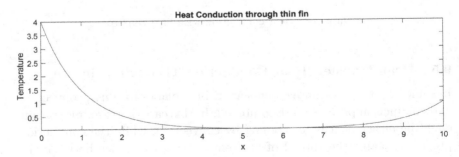

An interesting modification to this problem includes a source of heat generation Q such that

$$K\frac{d^2T}{dx^2} - hT = Q.$$

An application of this problem is heat sinks designed to protect computer hardware.

9.6 Heat Transfer: Ablation

Ablation combines convection and conduction in a solid and occurs in many examples such as spacecraft reentry, fire protection materials and melting processes. To model ablation, we study the boundary value problem

$$K\frac{d^2T}{dx^2} - C\frac{dT}{dx} = 0, \quad T_\infty = 0, \quad T_{wall} = 1.$$

Here C is related to convection processes and K is related to conduction processes. Let $K = 1$. After discretization, the equation becomes

$$K\frac{T_{i+1} - 2T_i + T_{i-1}}{\Delta x^2} - C\frac{T_{i+1} - T_{i-1}}{2\Delta x} = 0,$$

and use the tridiagonal solver to obtain the numerical solution which is shown below. A plot of the numerical solution, together with the exact solution

$$\frac{T - T_\infty}{T_{wall} - T_\infty} = e^{-Cx},$$

is shown in the figure below.

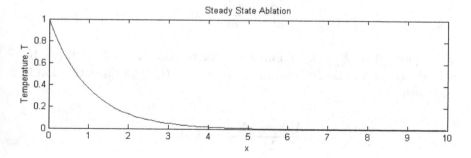

Figure 79: Ablation.

10. Chemical Reactions

In this section we will consider problems of simple one-step processes, as well as chemical oscillations and chemical chaos.

10.1   Chemical Reactions: One-Step Irreversible Reaction $A \rightarrow B$

Using the law of mass action, a differential equation is formulated for a one-step irreversible reaction $A \rightarrow B$, proceeding at rate k. The notation $[\cdot]$ denotes concentration, which takes a number between zero and one. The goal is to solve for the concentrations of reactant A forming product B at rate k using the initial concentration of A at time zero is one and B is zero, so $[A](0) = 1$ and $[B](0) = 0$. The equations are given by

$$\frac{d[A]}{dt} = -k[A]$$

$$\frac{d[B]}{dt} = k[A].$$

Note these equations are decoupled and one can just solve for the concentration of A. Adding together the differential equations gives

$$\frac{d[A]}{dt} + \frac{d[B]}{dt} = 0.$$

Therefore, $[A] + [B] = 1$, and an algebraic relation $[B] = 1 - [A]$ can be solved instead of the differential equation for $[B]$. The discretization is then just

$$\frac{[A]_{i+1} - [A]_i}{\Delta t} = -k[A]_i.$$

The solution found by numerical integration for $[A]$, then using the algebraic relationship to find $[B]$ is shown below.

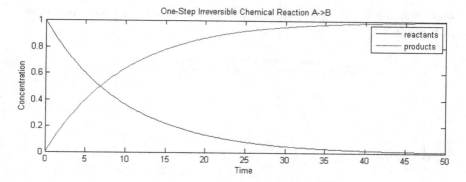

Figure 80:   One step irreversible reaction.

10.2   Chemical Reactions: Several Species

Consider a more general reversible chemical reaction involving 3 species of the form

$$A + B \underset{k_2}{\overset{k_1}{\rightleftarrows}} C.$$

Again, by the law of mass action, the system of differential equations is given by

$$\frac{d[A]}{dt} = -k_1[A][B] + k_2[C]$$

$$\frac{d[B]}{dt} = -k_1[A][B] + k_2[C]$$

$$\frac{d[C]}{dt} = k_1[A][B] - k_2[C].$$

In this case it is observed that all three chemical species tend to equilibrium after an initial transient period. Here the system is solved as a system of first order equations by discretizing as

$$\frac{[A]_{i+1} - [A]_i}{\Delta t} = -k_1[A]_i[B]_i + k_2[C]_i$$

$$\frac{[B]_{i+1} - [B]_i}{\Delta t} = -k_1[A]_i[B]_i + k_2[C]_i$$

$$\frac{[C]_{i+1} - [C]_i}{\Delta t} = k_1[A]_i[B]_i - k_2[C]_i,$$

and then solving for $[A], [B]$, and $[C]$ by the method for system shown in module 1.

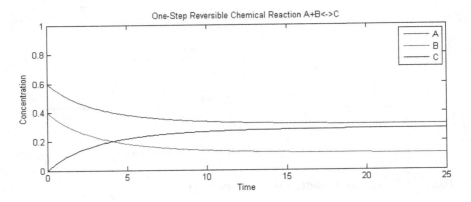

10.3   Chemical Oscillations: Belousov–Zhabotinsky Equations

Around 1950 Boris Belousov discovered chemical oscillations were possible by mixing citric acid in water, ceric ions and acidified bromate. Belousov's solution oscillated for about an hour before reaching equilibrium providing the first example of such a reaction, although now many oscillatory reactions are known. The result was viewed as preposterous by the mainstream chemical community and was essentially rejected outright until the work by Anatol Zhabotinsky 10 years later on the same reaction. Unfortunately for Belousov, he was only credited for his contribution after his death. In the mathematical model of this chemical mixing problem a Hopf bifurcation occurs. Here assume $a > 0$ the chemical mixing equations are given by

$$\frac{dx}{dt} = a - x - \frac{4xy}{1 + x^2}$$

$$\frac{dy}{dt} = bx\left(1 - \frac{y}{1 + x^2}\right)$$

for two mixing chemicals x and y. Choosing $a = 10$ and $b = 4$ produces a spiral, while choosing $a = 10$ and $b = 2$ produces a stable limit cycle. The dots are the initial conditions, and the trajectories in phase space are shown.

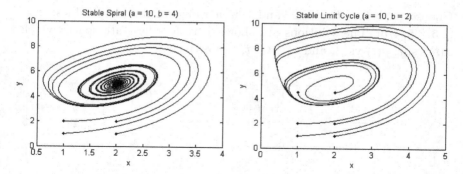

Figure 81: Belousov–Zhabotinsky reaction.

10.4 Chemical Chaos: Rossler Equations

A famous example of chemical reactions with chaotic behavior is given by the Rossler model

$$\frac{dx}{dt} = -y - z$$

$$\frac{dy}{dt} = x + ay$$

$$\frac{dz}{dt} = b + z(x - c).$$

Here we used the predictor-corrector method. First we solved for the predicted values $\bar{x}, \bar{y}$ and $\bar{z}$ using the dicretization for first order systems

$$\frac{\bar{x} - x_i}{\Delta t} = -y_i - z_i$$

$$\frac{\bar{y} - y_i}{\Delta t} = x_i + ay_i$$

$$\frac{\bar{z} - z_i}{\Delta t} = b + z_i(x_i - c).$$

Then, we performed the correction step

$$\frac{x_{i+1} - x_i}{\Delta t} = \frac{1}{2}(-y_i - z_i) + \frac{1}{2}(-\bar{y} - \bar{z})$$

$$\frac{y_{i+1} - y_i}{\Delta t} = \frac{1}{2}(x_i + ay_i) + \frac{1}{2}(\bar{x} + a\bar{y})$$

$$\frac{z_{i+1} - z_i}{\Delta t} = \frac{1}{2}(b + z_i(x_i - c)) + \frac{1}{2}(b + \bar{z}(\bar{x} - c)).$$

Choose $a = 0.2$, $b = 0.2$, and c is a range of different values: $c = [2.5, 3.5, 4, 5]$. The solutions are shown here for the state space, which $x(t)$ vs. t, $y(t)$ vs. t, and $z(t)$ vs. t, respectively.

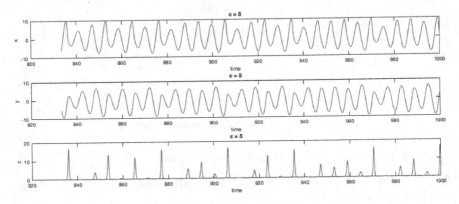

Figure 82:   Rossler system.

The phase space $x(t)$ vs. $y(t)$ vs. $z(t)$ is also shown, and the trajectory indicated is called a chaotic attractor.

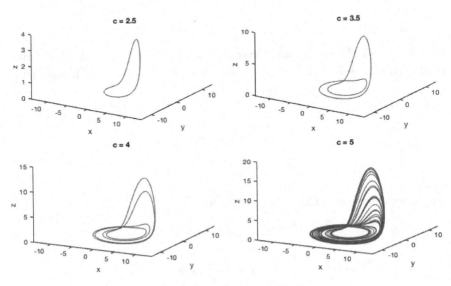

Figure 83:   Rossler chemical chaos.

11. Combustion

In this section we will consider thermal explosion theory, production of heat modeled by Arrhenius law, ignition based on Newton's cooling law, ignition based on Fourier cooling law, as well as solid propellant burning. In particular, the stability of these processes are studied numerically.

11.1 Combustion: Thermal Explosion Theory

Perhaps the simplest example of a thermal explosion model is given by the equation

$$\dot{u} = 1 + u^n.$$

For the special case when $n = 2$ the integral is elementary and has solutions for $-\pi/2 < t < \pi/2$:

$$u(t) = \tan(t) + c.$$

This is an example of solutions with finite time blow-up. Thermal explosion has important applications in mining, while the next several sections dealing with ignition are important in propulsion systems.

11.2 Combustion: Ignition Based on Newton's Cooling Law

This model of thermal ignition considers convection by Newton's Law, for small size propellant. The model of the ignition phenomena assumes that the steady-state temperature depends on heat production and losses. The combustion law is given for a temperature $T(t)$ with parameters: h, α, and β as:

$$T_t = -h(T - T_\infty) + \alpha e^{-\beta/T}.$$

Physically: h is the thermal conductivity, α is reaction exothermicity, and β is activation energy. We discretize this equation explicitly as

$$T^{k+1} = T^k + \Delta t(-h(T^k - T_\infty) + \alpha e^{-\beta/T^k}).$$

There are equilibrium solutions at the intersections where:

$$\alpha e^{-\beta/T} = h(T - T_\infty).$$

We solved the initial value problem with the following conditions:

$$T_\infty = 1, \quad T(0) = 0.$$

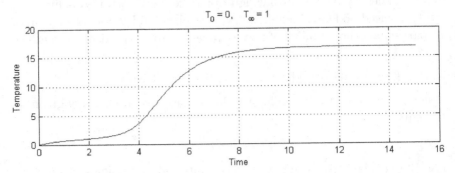

Figure 84: Example ignition solution for temperature profile as a function of time.

Solution of the initial value problem for a range of initial conditions.

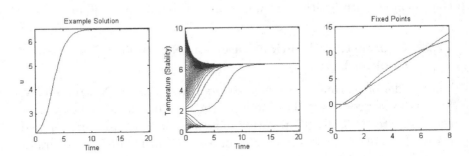

Figure 85: Ignition stability.

An important feature of this model is the scale on which temperature progresses from the initial value above the unstable fixed point and below the upper stable fixed point to the upper steady state. Conditioned on this region, this theory uses a steady state approach that is valid only when reaction and activation energy are large. Fortunately this is satisfied by many common applications validating the model.

11.3   Combustion: Ignition Based on Fourier's Conduction Law

This model of thermal ignition considers conduction by Fourier Law used for large propellant. The steady state theory is governed by the following equation

$$\nabla_r^2 u = -\delta e^u,$$

with appropriate boundary conditions. We solve the following three cases: flat slab $(n = 1)$, cylinder $(n = 2)$ and sphere $(n = 3)$, where n is the dimension.

For the flat slab:

$$u_{rr} + \delta e^u = 0.$$

For the cylinder:

$$\frac{1}{r}(ru_r)_r + \delta e^u = \frac{1}{r}u_r + u_{rr} + \delta e^u = 0.$$

For the sphere:

$$\frac{1}{r^2}(r^2 u_r)_r + \delta e^u = \frac{2}{r}u_r + u_{rr} + \delta e^u = 0.$$

We can generalize this formula as:

$$u_{rr} + \frac{n-1}{r}u_r + \delta e^u = 0$$

$$u(-1) = u(1) = 0, \quad u_r(0) = 0$$

where $n = 0, 1, 2$ respectively. This problem is axially symmetric, so the boundary conditions can be $u(-1) = u(1) = 0$, or the mixed boundary conditions $u(1) = 0$, $u_r(0) = 0$. This is a boundary value problem and central difference schemes are used to discretize the derivatives. The results are shown here plotting the value of δ vs $\beta = -\frac{du}{dr}(1)$ for a range of δ values. Notice that the equation is nonlinear, and for each value of δ the problem needs to be solved iteratively by lagging the nonlinear term and inverting a tridiagonal matrix using the Thomas algorithm (see the Appendix). This process is similar to what was discussed in Section 5.3.16.

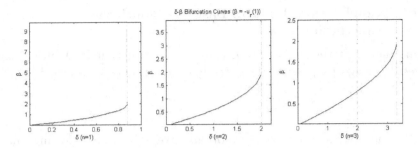

Figure 86:   Effect of geometry in thermal ignition.

Notice that the critical values for δ are $0.88, 2$, and 3.32 for the three geometries considered. For values of δ greater than the critical values, the solution will eventually blow up.

11.4   Combustion: Solid Propellant Burning

For solid propellant, the rate of change of combustion pressure is related to the accumulation of mass in the combustion chamber. For maximum flow rate per unit area (chocked flow), the amount of mass through the nozzle is proportional to the pressure in the combustion chamber. There is an equilibrium condition where the mass generated is equal to the mass that escapes. If more mass is generated than the mass that escapes, there will be a blow-up. The equilibrium state can be unstable or stable depending on the properties of the propellant and the operating conditions. As a simple model of this process, one can study the equation:

$$\frac{1}{p_e}\frac{dp}{dt} = c_1 p^n - c_2 p$$

where n is determined experimentally. Define p_e to be the equilibrium pressure. Given an initial pressure and value of $n < 1$, or $n > 1$, the pressure will go to p_e or to infinity.

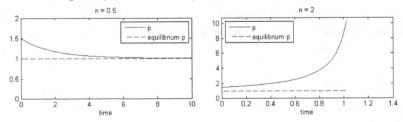

Figure 87:   Solid propellant burning.

PART III

Historical Biographies

12. Greek Mathematicians

1. Pythagoras of Samos (about 570–495 BCE)
2. Euclid of Alexandria (about 365–275 BCE)
3. Apollonius of Perga (about 262–190 BCE)
4. Archimedes of Syracuse (287–212 BCE)
5. Hero of Alexandria (about 10–70 CE)

12.1 Pythagoras of Samos (about 570–495 BCE)

Pythagoras is best known for the Pythagorean Theorem. The Pythagorean Theorem states that for any planar right triangle, the sum of the squares produced from the sides, a and b, of the right angle is equal to the square produced from the hypotenuse c, giving the famous equation

$$a^2 + b^2 = c^2.$$

Pythagoras founded one of the first institutions of higher learning, but unlike Plato's Academy, and Aristotle's Peripatetic School, the Pythagoreans are thought to have functioned more as a cultist and secretive society. The Pythagoreans believed that a number was the substance of all things, and are known for many observations about numbers, including: odd and even properties, perfect squares, tri-

"There is geometry in the humming of the strings, there is music in the spacing of the spheres."

angular numbers, and so on. There is much speculation about the life and dealings of Pythagoras, but the historical reality is that his true contribution has been lost or obscured over time. As Aristotle put it in his metaphysics "the so-called Pythagoreans, who were the first to take up mathematics, not only advanced this subject, but saturated with it, they fancied that the principles of mathematics were the principles of all things." In keeping with this, what is most clear about the life of Pythagoras is that he was a great scholar and devoted a good portion of his life to studying and advancing mathematics.

Pythagoras's main contribution to the present work is the Pythagorean Theorem which defines the distance between two points.

12.2   Euclid of Alexandria (about 365–275 BCE)

Euclid is best known for Euclidean Geometry and his most famous and enduring work *Elements*. Euclid is also credited with publishing several other works. Euclid also studied spherical geometry, number theory and mathematical rigor, such as proof writing. Today, more than two thousand years later, Euclid's *Elements* is still an authoritative reference on planar geometry. *Elements* built on and organized earlier work done by Thales, Pythagoras, Aristotle, Eudoxus, Plato, and others. Almost all of Euclid's *Elements* was already known to earlier mathematicians, and

"There is no royal road to geometry."

Euclid's main contribution is mainly thought to have been the compilation and clarification of the ideas, and especially the addition of rigorous proofs. *Elements* is divided into 13 books. Book 1 contains the 5 axioms and 5 postulates underpinning planar geometry. Euclid's axioms are:

1. Things which are equal to the same thing are also equal to one another.
2. If equals are added to equals, the wholes are equal.
3. If equals be subtracted from equals, the remainders are equal.
4. Things which coincide with one another are equal to one another.
5. The whole is greater than the part.

Euclid's postulates are:*

1. A straight line segment can be drawn joining any two points.
2. Any straight line segment can be extended indefinitely in a straight line.

---

*Axioms are self evident truths and should require little or no explanation. Postulates are not self evident, but they are assumed to be true, then from logical implication and deductive reasoning, a mathematical system will follow from the axioms and postulates.

3. To describe a circle with any center and distance.
4. All right angles are congruent.
5. If two lines are drawn which intersect a third in such a way that the sum of the inner angles on one side is less than two right angles, then the two lines must intersect each other on that side if extended far enough. This postulate is equivalent to what is known as the parallel postulate.

The parallel postulate, and particularly its relative complexity compared to the other postulates, led to great controversy among future mathematicians. The resolution of this controversy was not until János Bolyai (1802–1860) and Nikolai Lobachevsky (1792–1856) discovered that rejecting the parallel postulate led to the rigorous development of so-called non-Euclidean geometry. Many of the most well known and basic propositions of geometry, like the Pythagorean theorem, which is Proposition 47, are found in book 1. In Book 7, Euclid developed one of the first algorithms, which is a technique for finding the greatest common divisor of two numbers. In book 13, the Platonic solids and their properties are studied. The Platonic solids are regular, convex polyhedron with congruent faces of regular polygons, and the same number of faces meeting at each vertex. Just 5 solids meet the criteria, and each is named after its number of faces: Tetrahedron (Fire), Icosahedron (Water), Dodecahedron (Aether), Octahededron (Air), Hexahedron (Earth).

There are two famous anecdotes associated with Euclid that resonate for students of math and science. First, Ptolemy 1 (367–282 BCE), the Macedonian general of Alexander the Great (356–323 BCE) who became king and pharaoh of Egypt and funded *Elements*, apparently had great difficulty to learn it. Ptolomy asked Euclid if there was an easier way to learn it, and Euclid answered. "There is no royal road to geometry." Second, it is said that a student studying *Elements* asked Euclid "What shall I gain by learning this?," to which Euclid asked a slave to give the student a coin, "since he must make gain out of what he learns."

Euclid's main contribution to the present work is his 13 books on geometry.

12.3   Apollonius of Perga (about 262–190 BCE)

Apollonius was an astronomer and mathematician born in Perga, which is in modern day Turkey. Apollonius also researched the moon and planets, and a crater on the Moon is named in his honor. Apollonius, like many scholars of the day, is thought to have traveled to Alexandria, to study with the students of Euclid. Apollionius made major developments in the theory of conic sections which directly contributed to later work by Ptolemy, Kepler, Descartes, Newton and others. Although it is speculated he is responsible for several major works of mathematics, Apollonius is best known for his most famous work which is called *Conics*. *Conics* consisted of 8 books and some 387 mathematical propositions. In this work, Apollonius was the first

"Indeed I had put down everything just as it occurred to me, postponing revision until the end."

to name the ellipse, parabola, and hyperbola, and he was also the first to identify several properties of them. It is noted that Ptolemy (90–168 CE) describes Apollonius' theorem in the *Almagest*, which states for any triangle with corners A, B, C and where D is the midpoint of side BC, it follows

$$|AB|^2 + |AC|^2 = 2(|AD|^2 + |BD|^2).$$

For right triangles, this theorem is equivalent to the Pythagorean Theorem. Apollonius is also speculated to have studied circle packing problems, leading to the *Apollonian Gasket* being named in his honor (the following work done much later, especially by Descartes).

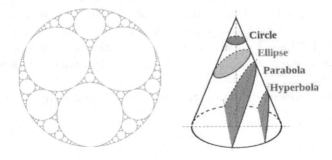

Figure 88:   Apollonius gasket (*left*) and conic sections (*right*).

Apollonius's main contribution to the present work is his book on conic sections.

12.4 Archimedes of Syracuse (287–212 BCE)

Archimedes contributed a staggering amount of original ideas to mathematics and engineering. Archimedes is generally regarded as the greatest mathematician and scientist of antiquity and one of the greatest mathematicians of all time (together with Isaac Newton, Leohnard Euler and Carl Friedrich Gauss). Many works are attributed to Archimedes: *On plane equilibriums, Quadrature of the parabola, On the sphere and cylinder, On spirals, On conoids and spheroids, Measurement of a circle, The Sandreckoner*, and *On the method of mechanical problems*. As recently as the

"Give me a lever and a place to stand and I will move the earth."

20th century, a Palimpsest was carefully recovered and translated containing the previously unknown works of Archimedes *The Method, Stomachion*, and *On Floating Bodies*. Archimedes is known for the law of the lever which goes with the famous quotation "give me the place to stand, and I shall move the earth." The law of the lever has a remarkably simple mathematical statement that says at equilibrium

$$m_1 \quad \overset{x_1 \qquad x_2}{\underset{\triangle}{\rule{6cm}{0.4pt}}} \quad m_2 \qquad m_1 x_1 = m_2 x_2$$

where m_1 and m_2 are masses supported on a rigid beam of length $x_1 + x_2$ with a fulcrum placed x_1 distance from mass m_1 and x_2 distance from mass m_2. Archimedes is also known for the principle of buoyancy, which explains that a body immersed in a fluid experiences a buoyant force equal to the weight of the fluid it displaces. This principle is associated with the famous quotation "Eureka, I found it!" This story is told in regard to detection of fraud in the manufacture of a golden crown commissioned by Hiero II, the king of Syracuse. The king weighed out the gold, and gave it to a goldsmith to be made into a crown, but suspected he was cheated by the goldsmith and commissioned Archimedes to investigate.

Archimedes is also known for the method of exhaustion to estimate areas and volumes, which is similar to the Riemann sum quadrature used in modern integral calculus. This technique is closely related to finding the sums of infinite series, very often a complicated problem even for 21st century mathematicians. Using the Method of Exhaustion, Archimedes made at the time a very accurate approximation of π using 96 sided polygons to achieve $3\frac{10}{71} < \pi < 3\frac{1}{7}$. This approximation gives $\pi \approx 3.14185110$. Another achievement of Archimedes was construction of the Archimedean Spiral where

$$r = a + b\theta^{1/c}$$

for constants a, b, and c (typically $c = 1$), such that the distance between turnings is constant. Archimedes discovered that the volume of a sphere is $2/3$ the volume of a cylinder enclosing it. Archimedes actually wanted this on his tombstone thinking it was his greatest achievement. Historically, beyond his mathematical achievements, Archimedes was a feared and respected military and industrial inventor. It is said he invented a claw-like lever to attack ships in defense of Syracuse against Roman sieges, catapults, and optical defenses using mirrors that concentrate sunlight. He also invented a water screw, that was useful for agriculture.

Figure 89:   Ship claw (*top*) and water screw (*bottom*).

The death of Archimedes is a famously sad story, where the commanding general Marcellus of an attacking Roman army in the siege of Syracuse had ordered Archimedes specifically to not be harmed out of great respect for his machines that had killed so many of his men. However, he was murdered in cold blood for ignoring, and thereby disrespecting, a Roman soldier who demanded his name while he was in private study. As the soldier made to kill him, stepping forward into the geometric drawings that commanded his full attention, "do not disturb my circles," is thought to have been his last words.

Archimedes contribution to the present work is his method of exhaustion to calculate the areas under curves.

12.5 Hero of Alexandria (about 10–70 CE)

Little is known about the life of Hero, or Heron, of Alexandria. His life is known almost entirely from his numerous surviving works: *Automata, Barulkos, Belopoiica, Catoptrica, Cheirobalistra, Definitiones, Dioptra, Geometrica, Mechanica, De mensuris, Metrica, Pneumatica,* and *Stereometrica.* He is best known for two major contributions, one in mathematics and one in engineering. To mathematics, is Hero's formula for computing the area, A, of an arbitrary planar triangle given its side lengths a, b, c :

$$A = \sqrt{s(s-a)(s-b)(s-c)},$$

where $s = \frac{a+b+c}{2}$. This formula is a special case of Brahmagupta's formula for the area of a cyclic quadrilateral, published by the Indian mathematician and astronomer Brahmagupta (598–670 CE). It is also believed to have been independently discovered by the Chinese and was published in "Mathematical Treatise in Nine Sections," by Qin Jiushao (circa 1247 CE). Second, Hero of Alexandria invented what is called Heron's aeolipile. The aeolipile is regarded as the first steam engine and earliest example of a primitive jet engine.

Figure 90: Hero's aeolipile.

It was written by the Greek mathematician Pappus (290–350 CE), describing the contributions of Heron in Book VIII of his *Mathematical Collection* "the mechanicians of Heron's school say that mechanics can be divided into a theoretical and a manual part; the theoretical part is composed of geometry, arithmetic, astronomy and physics, the manual is work in metals, architecture, carpentering and painting and anything involving skill with the hands." This is a useful distinction that even today arguably remains just as valid.

Hero of Alexandria's contribution to the present work is Aeolipile which is the first application of the concept of jet propulsion.

13. Pioneers in Mathematics

1. René Descartes (1596–1650)
2. Christian Huygens (1629–1695)

3. Isaac Newton (1643–1727)
4. Gottfried Wilhelm Leibniz (1646–1716)
5. Leonhard Euler (1707–1783)
6. Daniel Bernoulli (1700–1782)
7. Carl Friedrich Gauss (1777–1855)
8. Georg Friedrich Bernhard Riemann (1826–1866)

13.1 René Descartes (1596–1650)

Descartes was a French philosopher, mathematician, and scientist who is actually best
known for his many and significant contributions to western philosophy. He was a law student and later a soldier. Descartes is known
for his metaphysical studies where he contem-
plated existence, and is particularly remembered for his observation in *Discours de la
méthode* which contains the phrase "cogito,
ergo sum" meaning "I think, therefore I am."
Descartes also had a strong influence on mathematics with his concept and clear description
of what is now called the Cartesian coordinate

"I think, therefore I am."

system published in his work *La Géométrie*. Descartes is also credited with
several other important mathematical advancements. He developed a rule
of signs for polynomials that can be useful for determining their limiting
behavior and roots. He also did pioneering work finding normal and tangent
lines to curves that set the foundation for the Calculus to be later success-
fully developed by Newton and Leibniz. In algebra, he helped invent and
popularize the use of exponent notation, i.e. x^5. For his many contributions
to both areas of mathematics, Descartes is sometimes thought of as the
"father of analytical geometry," which is the intersection of geometry and
algebra.

Descartes's contributions to the present work is his Cartesian coordinates and analytic geometry.

13.2   Christian Huygens (1629–1695)

Huygens was a Dutch mathematician and physicist. Huygens made extensive contributions to many areas of science, including astronomy and engineering. Huygens made pioneering studies on pendulums and had a major impact on the development of horology, which is the study of clocks and keeping time. Huygens studied probability theory, and did pioneering work there in his work "On Reasoning in Games of Chance." Huygens made observations about Saturn's rings and discovered Saturn's moon Titan. The European Space Agency (ESA), named a spacecraft that landed on Titan in 2005 after him.

"I believe that we do not know anything for certain, but everything probably."

    The main contribution of Huygens to the present work is his study of pendulums.

13.3   Isaac Newton (1643–1727)

Isaac Newton possessed one of the finest and most disciplined minds of all time, and contributed a staggering amount of original and important research to science and mathematics, as well as other fields. Isaac Newton made numerous groundbreaking discoveries as a mathematician and scientist (particularly in optics and mechanics), and he also made extensive research efforts in Theology and Alchemy during his life. Newton is perhaps best known for Newtonian Mechanics, which is still the best theory to describe the physics of motion except in certain special or extreme

"Truth is ever to be found in the simplicity, and not in the multiplicity and confusion of things."

cases, such as viscoelastic fluids or relativistic travel velocities. Newton is also known for his work *Optics*, which included the theory of light and color, his design of scientific instruments (esp. reflector telescope), a study of dynamics, and particularly his universal law of gravitation which states the attraction force F_g is given by

$$F_g = \frac{GmM}{r^2}$$

where m and M are two masses, r is the distance between their centers and G is gravitational constant. Newton's success in particular with the law of gravitation was an achievement that many other eminent scholars of the day, including Robert Hooke, Edmund Halley, and others had attempted without success.

The number of major concepts in mathematics and physics named after Newton is large. In particular, for the present work the focus is on a few: Newton-Cotes Formulas (trapezoidal rule, which is a special case), Newton Series (more commonly called finite differences), Newton's Constant (G the gravitational constant), Newton's Method, Newton's Law of Cooling, Newton's Laws of Motion, Newton's Cannon, and Newton's Fluid Viscosity Law. All these represent just a small selection of Newton's vast contributions. Newton was a very hard worker, and was also a deeply religious person and carried out extensive theological researches rivaling his work in mathematics and physics. Newton's work *Philosophiae Naturalis Principia Mathematica* in 1687 is generally regarded as one of the greatest scientific works ever. In this study, Newton explained planetary motion and universal gravitation and set out what are today called "Newton's laws." Newton's vast mathematical contributions also include power series and binomial theorem, and the fundamental theorem of calculus, applications to extrema problems, area problems, and algorithms for the use of calculus.

In reflecting on Newton's contributions, it is difficult to imagine how one person could have done so much work in a lifetime. Newton was noticed to be very good at school and reading early on and his uncle suggested he go to Cambridge University (Trinity). Newton started at 19, graduated at 23, got a masters in 1667 at 25 and became a professor at 27. After his adviser Isaac Barrow (1630–1677), he was the second Lucasian Professor of Mathematics (a prestigious professorship held at Cambridge University). Newton was admitted to the Royal Society, and later went on to be its president in 1703 — a position which he arguably abused to some extent in favoring his own works and discrediting that of his competitors (like Hooke and Leibniz). It is generally agreed that Newton developed calculus before Gottfried Wilhelm Leibniz. It is also however generally agreed that

Leibniz developed it independently, since Leibniz published first in 1684. A fight of priority for this momentous discovery developed into a small war that ultimately consumed Newton and discredited and ruined Leibniz to the extent he was outcast and buried in an unmarked grave. Later in his life Newton became Master of the Mint, Justice of the Peace, and he was also a member of parliament at one point. Lagrange wrote "Newton was the greatest genius that ever existed."

Newton's contribution to the present work is primarily the invention of calculus and particularly the fundamental theorem of calculus, Newton's method, the laws of motion, gravitational law, Newton's viscosity law, and Newton's cooling law.

13.4   Gottfried Wilhelm Leibniz (1646–1716)

Leibniz is best known as a philosopher, and for his work on the Calculus. It is generally agreed Newton developed calculus before Leibniz, but that Leibniz developed it independently. There was a great priority dispute between Leibniz and Newton over the calculus. It is important to recognize though not only were their notational differences in their descriptions of the Calculus, there were also major theoretical differences. For example, Newton was interested in motion and physical matter, while Leibniz focused more on algorithms, algebraic ideas, rules for integration and differentiation. Leibniz published his work on calculus first in 1684, and received a great

"When a truth is necessary, the reason for it can be found by analysis."

amount of fame and recognition for this achievement. However, Newton had made the discovery in 1664–1666 and immediately accused Leibniz of plagiarism. This accusation was settled by trial, and ultimately a Royal Society Commission was appointed to settle the dispute. As president of the Royal Society at the time, not only did Newton, in a breathtaking display of corruption, personally chair the commission, but he also wrote the majority opinion for the court. Such was the power and fame of Isaac Newton that Leibniz spent the last few years of his life in a war with Newton and others trying to prove he developed Calculus independently. When Leibniz died most of Europe thought he basically copied Newton, he was labeled a fraud and was immensely unpopular. His reputation has been growing since then to the modern day, and to Leibniz's great credit and ultimate victory, not only do we still use his notation for calculus today, but it is widely believed the English mathematics fell behind mainland Europe due to the complexity and difficulty of Newton's poor notation and their absolute insistence on adhering to it (such was the influence of Newton even after his death).

Leibniz had notable achievements in several other areas, which included statics and dynamics, conservation of kinetic energy, and mechanical calculators. The Leibniz wheel is one of the first mechanical calculators. Leibniz's vast body of work is distributed throughout published works, as well as many unpublished works and private letters.

Liebniz contribution to the present work is his invention of calculus and particularly the fundamental theorem of calculus, and also the first mechanical calculator.

13.5   Leonhard Euler (1707–1783)

Laplace once said "Read Euler: he is our master in everything." The contributions of Euler are so numerous, and of such great importance, it is difficult to summarize them and their influence. Euler worked in just about every known area of mathematics and he even essentially founded new areas of mathematics, like topology for example. His research efforts had lasting influence in the natural sciences as well.

Euler was born in Basel, Switzerland, and was recognized as a very gifted youth with a tremendous memory, facility for languages and ability to calculate things in his head. An example of his calculating abilities, albeit one from later in his life, is his proof in 1772 that $2^{31} - 1 = 2,147,483,647$ is a Mersenne prime. This number was the largest known prime for almost 100 years. At 13 years old he entered

"For since the fabric of the universe is most perfect and the work of a most wise Creator, nothing at all takes place in the universe in which some rule of maximum or minimum does not appear."

the University of Basel where he met Johann Bernoulli (1667–1748), probably the greatest mathematician in the world at the time, who was a professor there. Bernoulli to some extent coached Euler and even allowed him private meetings weekly to ask his questions. Euler graduated with a master degree in philosophy in 1720, and in 1726 completed a dissertation on the theory of sound.

With the help of Daniel Bernoulli, after a few troubles finding a job, Euler eventually was hired as a physics professor at the Imperial Russian Academy of Sciences in St. Petersburg, where he eventually became head of the mathematics department in 1733. By around 1738 Euler had nearly lost his eyesight, but it did not slow his research. In 1741, Euler moved to Germany and became a professor at the Berlin Academy. He remained in Berlin until around 1766 when he moved back to Russia taking a position at the St. Petersburg Academy, where he remained until he died in 1783. Euler was the first to think of the modern concept of a function $f(x)$. He also invented e for the base of the natural logarithm, sigma notation for sums, and i for the imaginary number $\sqrt{-1}$. Euler solved several problems in power series, the most famous being, what is today called, the Basel problem

$$\sum_{n=1}^{\infty} \frac{1}{n^2} = \frac{\pi^2}{6}.$$

This number theory problem was first studied by Pietro Mengoli (1626–1686) in 1644, and it was not until 1735 that the correct solution was found. Euler also proved Euler's Identity

$$e^{i\theta} = \cos\theta + i\sin\theta$$

which gives the remarkable formula

$$e^{i\pi} + 1 = 0.$$

Forward and backward Euler method are finite difference methods for solving differential equations. For example, solving $dy/dt = y$, the equation can be approximated using

1. Forward Euler

$$\frac{y_n - y_{n-1}}{\Delta x} = y_{n-1}$$

2. Backward Euler

$$\frac{y_n - y_{n-1}}{\Delta x} = y_n$$

Other contributions are: Euler line, Euler Circle, Euler Characteristic, Euler Number, Euler formula, Euler Analytical Method for linear differential equations, Euler-Cauchy Equations, Euler Discretization Method, Euler-Lagrange Equation in calculus of variations, Euler Angles, and equations of rigid body dynamics and spin stabilization, Euler Frame, Euler Equations of Fluid Mechanics, Proof of Bernoulli's law for steady inviscid incompressible flow, Euler-Bernoulli Beam, Euler loads, buckling problems, and other contributions to solid mechanics, Euler-Maclaurin formula, Euler total derivative, and formulas for the coefficients of Fourier series.

The main contributions of Euler to the present work are the exponential function, the number e, Euler Formula, Euler scheme based on forward and backward differences, Euler analytical methods for solving linear differential equations with constant coefficients (assuming the solution to be exponential function with unknown exponent), bending and buckling analysis, and Euler equations of fluid mechanics.

13.6 Daniel Bernoulli (1700–1782)

Daniel Bernoulli was a mathematician and physicist, and was one of several prominent Bernoulli family scholars. Bernoulli is probably best known for his Bernoulli's Law of fluid mechanics

$$\frac{1}{2}u^2 + \frac{p}{\rho} = \text{constant}.$$

Bernoulli's principle states that for an inviscid nonconducting fluid, as the velocity increases the pressure decreases. Bernoulli is also known for his collaboration with Euler in developing the Euler–Bernoulli beam equation

$$\frac{\mathrm{d}^2}{\mathrm{d}x^2}\left(EI\frac{\mathrm{d}^2v}{\mathrm{d}x^2}\right) = -w$$

which describes a beam's deflection under a load. Here $v(x)$ is the deflection, E is the elastic modulus, I is the second moment of inertia, and w is the load. Euler and Bernoulli were

"There is no philosophy which is not founded upon knowledge of the phenomena, but to get any profit from this knowledge it is absolutely necessary to be a mathematician."

not only working colleagues, they were also friends, and Euler married Bernoulli's sister.

The main contributions of Bernoulli to the present work are Bernoulli's Law, the most famous equation in fluid mechanics, and also Bernoulli's Euler-Beam Equation.

13.7   Carl Friedrich Gauss (1777–1855)

It is sometimes said that Newton was the greatest mathematician of the 17th century, Euler of the 18th and Gauss of the 19th. Gauss proved the fundamental theorem of algebra for his dissertation in 1799, which basically states that every polynomial of degree n with complex coefficients (which thus also includes real coefficients) has exactly n roots, counting multiplicity. Several other prominent mathematicians, such as Euler, Lagrange, d'Alembert and Laplace, had previously failed in their attempts to prove this theorem. It turns out that Gauss's proof also contained an omission that was not corrected until 1920 by Alexander Ostrowski. Gaussian Elimination is the classical algorithm for solving linear algebra problems of the form $Ax = b$. Other efforts

"When a philosopher says something that is true then it is trivial. When he says something that is not trivial then it is false."

from scholars like Cayley, Euler and Sylvester, used matrices, but Gauss used his theory to solve systems of equations directly. Gauss's method is still the most effective method. The Gaussian Distribution is a fundamental contribution in probabilty. Gauss also made important contributions to astronomy. Gauss is credited with developing the least squares method. Gauss is sometimes called the Prince of Algebra.

The main contributions of Gauss to the present work are the fundamental theorem of algebra (quadratic equation has two roots counting multiplicity), Gaussian elimination, and Gauss divergence theorem of vector analysis.

13.8   Georg Friedrich Bernhard Riemann (1826–1866)

Bernhard Riemann worked primarily on analysis, number theory and differential geometry. His many contributions have had a profound effect on mathematics and physics. Riemann is probably best known for his work in prime number theory and what is today still an open problem called the "Riemann Hypothesis," which is currently considered one of the greatest unsolved problems in mathematics. In his work titled *On the number of primes less than a given magnitude*, Riemann connected the distribution of prime numbers to the zeros of the Riemann zeta function. Euler

"If only I had the theorems! Then I should find the proofs easily enough."

once wrote of problems like this that "mathematicians have tried in vain to this day to discover some order in the sequence of prime numbers, and we have reason to believe that it is a mystery into which the human mind will never penetrate." Riemann also made extensive contributions to calculus and analysis by developing Riemann sums and the Riemann Integral, which are a rigorous way of defining a definite integral over a closed region. Riemann also made extensive progress in the theory of trigonometric series by giving criterion under which a function could be represented as a Fourier Series. Riemann's work in differential geometry, and the development of what is called Riemannian Geometry, proved very important in mathematical physics and for the study of general relativity. Riemann is also known for solving what is today called the Riemann problem of gas dynamics.

The main contribution of Riemann to the present work is Riemann sum in calculus and his work on gas dynamics.

14. French School of Mathematics

1. Pierre de Fermat (1601–1665)
2. Blaise Pascal (1623–1662)
3. Pierre-Simon Laplace (1749–1827)
4. Augustin Louis Cauchy (1789–1857)
5. Jean-Baptiste Joseph Fourier (1768–1830)
6. Jean le Rond d'Alembert (1717–1783)
7. Siméon Denis Poisson (1781–1840)
8. Joseph-Louis Lagrange (1736–1813)
9. Jules Henri Poincaré (1854–1912)

14.1 Pierre de Fermat (1601–1665)

Fermat was a lawyer and mathematician. Fermat is credited by Newton and Leibniz for having done essential foundational work leading up to the infinitesimal calculus. Fermat's original work in this area was published in *Methodus ad disquirendam maximam et minima* and in *De tangentibus linearum curvarum*. As the titles of the works indicate, Fermat used this method to find maxima and minima, as well as tangent lines to curves. Similar developments were made by Descartes, who was a critic of Fermat at the time. Fermat is best known for Fermat's Last Theorem, which he described in a note at the margin of a copy of Diophantus' *Arithmetica*

"I have found a very great number of exceedingly beautiful theorems."

$$x^n + y^n = z^n, \text{ where } n \geq 3, \text{ has no solutions with } x, y, z \in \mathbb{N}.$$

Fermat wrote "I discovered a truly remarkable proof of this theorem which this margin is too small to contain." The theorem was finally proved around 1995, primarily by Andrew Wiles, but with the help of Richard Taylor after an error was discovered in Wiles' manuscript during peer review. It is very unlikely that Fermat had a genuine proof of the theorem.

Fermat also made notable contributions to analytic geometry, probability, and optics. Fermat's contributions include early ideas about the

Principle of Least Action, in particular via Snell's Law of Refraction and the observation that light will follow a path to minimize the travel time. This study, the result sometimes being called Fermat's Principle, was an early example of using a variational principle. Fermat is also credited, along with his collaborator Blaise Pascal, as a pioneer in probability theory.

The main contributions of Fermat to the present work is his early development of calculus, tangent lines, and the law of least action which is important in dynamics.

14.2   Blaise Pascal (1623–1662)

Blaise Pascal was a French mathematician, and he also made contributions to physics and philosophy. Pascal is known for Pascal's Triangle which can be used to determine the coefficients of binomial expansions (terms that have the form $(x + y)^n$, for any $n \in \mathbb{N}$), among other things. It should be noted that Yang Hui (960–1279 CE) discovered this triangle well before Pascal. Some of Pascal's most significant work was done on probability theory in collaboration with Fermat. This early work on probability theory was some of the first work ever done in the field. Pascal also had several important contributions to fluid dynamics, the most important being Pascal's Law which can be formulated as

"I have only made this letter longer because I have not had the time to make it shorter."

$$\Delta p = \rho g(\Delta h),$$

for the change in pressure p, density ρ, gravity g and columnar height h of a fluid. This law states that a pressure force exerted in an incompressible confined fluid propagates equally in all directions, and is the essential mathematical principle at work for a hydraulic press. This contribution expands on work done by Evangelista Torricelli (1608–1647) and Daniel Bernoulli. Pascal is also credited with inventing the syringe, and making a mechanical calculator, later called a Pascaline, that was capable of addition and subtraction. The *Pascal* is the SI unit of pressure, and is a popular programming language.

In 1654 it is said that Pascal had a severe religious experience that caused him to give up mathematics and natural philosophy and to focus entirely on theology. In fact, Pascal is arguably best known as a philosopher, especially for his famous wager argument as a reason to believe in God. The core argument of Pascal's Wager, which basically tries to give a game theoretic reason for why belief in God is simply the logical choice to make. As put forth in his work *Pensées*, the argument states "If you gain, you gain all; if you lose, you lose nothing."

The main contributions of Pascal to the present work are his theorem on pressure in fluids as a state variable, and the unit of pressure Pascal is N/m^2.

14.3 Pierre-Simon, marquis de Laplace (1749–1827)

Laplace was a French polymath that made so many important contributions across the sciences, especially in mathematics and physics, that he is sometimes called the "Newton of France." Like Newton and Euler, there are many important discoveries that bear Laplace's name. Laplace's major work *Mécanique Céleste* (Celestial Mechanics) improved on Newton's *Principia*. Laplace also made some developments regarding the speed of sound as it relates to air temperature and pressure via the heat capacity ratio γ where

$$\gamma = \frac{c_p}{c_v}$$

"Such is the advantage of a well-constructed language that its simplified notation often becomes the source of profound theories."

and c_p is the specific heat at constant pressure and c_v is the specific heat at constant volume. This contribution is related to the propagation of noise and states the speed of sound in an ideal gas as given by

$$c = \sqrt{\frac{\gamma p}{\rho}}.$$

Note that the speed of sound is a function of temperature, and increases with increasing temperature. An interesting story connected to this property is a mistake made by Newton when he assumed that the process is isothermal, attributing discrepancies in his calculations to the foggy weather in London, a mistake Laplace did not repeat. Laplace also developed an early theory of capillary action which describes how fluid surface tension and adhesion can cause a fluid to flow even in very narrow ducts. Laplace is credited with being one of the first people to apply Bayesian methods, an advancement in probability theory that is difficult to overstate the importance of. Laplace's principle of insufficient reason is still a major cornerstone of Bayesian statistics theory.

The main contribution of Laplace to the present work is his derivation of the speed of sound $a^2 = \gamma p/\rho = \gamma RT$, assuming isentropic conditions (correcting Newton's derivation, who had assumed isothermal conditions).

14.4 Augustin Louis Cauchy (1789–1857)

Augustin Cauchy was a prominent French mathematician, engineer and physicist, who is known for many important contributions. In fact, the number of mathematical and scientific ideas named after Cauchy rivals that of any other person in history. Cauchy made important contributions in algebra and group theory, optics, elasticity, mathematical physics, and differential equations. Cauchy is one of the primary figures that introduced modern rigor into mathematical analysis. Cauchy's work *Cours d'Analyse* in 1821 was one of the first studies of complex analysis. A complex numbers $z \in \mathbb{Z}$ is given as

"Very often the laws derived by physicists from a large number of observations are not rigorous, but approximate."

$$z = a + bi$$

where, $a, b \in \mathbb{R}$ and $i = \sqrt{-1}$. Cauchy explained operations with complex numbers, and many results with complex functions including the treatment of improper integrals and limits. The Cauchy test for checking the convergence or divergence of infinite series is a particularly useful result which states that a series $\sum_{i=0}^{\infty} x_i$ is convergent if and only if for every $\epsilon > 0$ there exists a natural number N such that $|x_n - x_m| < \epsilon$ whenever $n, m > N$.

The main contribution of Cauchy to the present work is his rigorous analysis of calculus.

14.5   Jean-Baptiste Joseph Fourier (1768–1830)

Joseph Fourier was a mathematician and physicist best known for his work on trigonometric series. The Fourier Series is given by

$$(S_N f)(x) = \frac{a_0}{2} + \sum_{n=1}^{N} [a_n \cos(nx)$$
$$+ b_n \sin(nx)], \quad N \geq 0,$$

which is an infinite series of trigonometric functions that represents an approximation of a periodic function $f(x)$ which improves as N goes to infinity. For a periodic function $f(x)$ that is integrable on $[-\pi, \pi]$, where

$$a_n = \frac{1}{\pi} \int_{-\pi}^{\pi} f(x) \cos(nx) dx, \quad n \geq 0$$

and

"Primary causes are unknown to us; but are subject to simple and constant laws."

$$b_n = \frac{1}{\pi} \int_{-\pi}^{\pi} f(x) \sin(nx) dx, \quad n \geq 1$$

are called the Fourier coefficients of $f(x)$. The Fourier Series, and also the Fourier Transform, has many applications in science and engineering.

Fourier also published several early results studying heat and thermodynamics. Other major developments leading up to this idea were contributed by Euler, d'Alembert, Bernoulli and others. Fourier also made important contributions to heat flow in his work *The Analytic Theory of Heat*. From this work, we have Fourier's law of heat conduction which can be stated in one-dimension as

$$q = -k \frac{dT}{dx}$$

where q is heat flux per unit area, k is the material conductivity, and T is the temperature. Fourier is also generally credited with the discovery of the greenhouse effect. Fourier was also the analysis teacher of Claude Navier at École Polytechnique, and served as a teacher and mentor for him. Fourier was also a science adviser of Napoleon Bonaparte and went on expedition with him to Egypt in 1798.

The main contributions of Fourier to the present work are Fourier Series and Fourier law of heat conduction.

14.6   Jean le Rond d'Alembert (1717–1783)

D'Alembert was a French mathematician, engineer, physicist, philosopher and enthusiast of music. D'Alembert was known for contributions to dynamics. He is also known for many scientific advances, but in particular d'Alembert solution to the wave equation, and d'Alembert's Paradox. He is probably best known for D'Alembert's Formula for obtaining solutions to the wave equation. In flight sciences and fluid mechanics, d'Alembert's Paradox states that for incompressible and inviscid potential flow there is zero net force on a body moving with constant velocity relative to the fluid. This result does not match with experimental data which suggests the drag force cannot be zero. This issue was not

"Of all the great men of antiquity, Archimedes may be the one who most deserves to be placed beside Homer."

resolved until 1904 when the German engineer Ludwig Prandtl provided the key insight that a very thin viscous boundary layer is present.

The main contributions of d'Alembert to the present work is d'Alembert paradox.

14.7   Siméon Denis Poisson (1781–1840)

Poisson was a prolific scientist and mathematician. In mathematics Poisson studied calculus, especially integrals and series, mathematical physics, probability theory, and differential equations. He is especially regarded for Poisson's Equation, which extends the work of Laplace and has many applications. Poisson was the first to derive the isentropic relation (i.e. adiabatic and reversible process)

$$\frac{p}{p_1} = \left(\frac{\rho}{\rho_1}\right)^{\gamma}$$

and it is called Poisson's adiabat. Also, the ratio of the lateral strain to the axial strain of

"That which can affect our senses in any manner whatever, is termed matter."

a wire is known as Poisson's Ratio. Similar ratios appear in stress-strain relations of plates as well.

The main contribution of Poisson to the present work is Poisson's adiabat.

14.8   Joseph-Louis Lagrange (1736–1813)

Lagrange was an influential and respected mathematician and astronomer who not only made several important contributions, but he did much to clarify these subjects. In a very telling analysis of Lagrange's work, the esteemed mathematical history scholar W.W. Rouse Ball (1850–1925) wrote "The great masters of modern analysis are Lagrange, Laplace, and Gauss, who were contemporaries. It is interesting to note the marked contrast in their styles. Lagrange is perfect both in form and matter, he is careful to explain his procedure, and though his arguments are general they are easy to follow. Laplace on the other hand explains nothing, is indifferent to style, and, if satisfied that his results are correct, is content to leave them either with no proof or with a faulty one. Gauss is as exact and elegant as Lagrange, but even more difficult to follow than Laplace, for he removes

"As long as algebra and geometry proceeded along separate paths, their advance was slow and their applications limited. But when these sciences joined company, they drew from each other fresh vitality and thenceforward marched on at a rapid pace toward perfection."

every trace of the analysis by which he reached his results, and studies to give a proof which while rigorous shall be as concise and synthetical as possible."

Lagrange's treatise on analytical mechanics *Mécanique Analytique* was the most significant work in classical mechanics since Newton's *Principia*. In what is today called Lagrangian mechanics, Lagrange also developed a completely new system of mechanics based on the calculus of variations and the principle of least action.

The main contribution of Lagrange to the present work is his Lagrangian dynamics which is an alternative to Newton's dynamics.

14.9 Jules Henri Poincaré (1854–1912)

Henri Poincaré was a French mathematician, physicist and polymath. He is probably most famous for the Poincaré conjecture, which remained unsolved until Russian Grigori Perelman finished the proof in 2003. This theorem is a topology result. Poincaré along with Edward Norton Lorenz (1917–2008) is one of the early pioneers of modern chaos theory and discovered sensitivity to initial conditions (SIC) in his work on the three body problem. Poincaré invented the stability classification for dynamical systems: saddle, center, node, spiral, etc. By linearizing systems of nonlinear first order ordinary differential equations about their steady states, Poincaré developed a methodology to make a qualitative analysis of the solution space.

"It is by logic that we prove, but by intuition that we discover. To know how to criticize is good, to know how to create is better."

The Poincaré-Bendixson theorem, also named after Ivar Otto Bendixson (1861–1935), is an important result in dynamical system theory. We should mention, in this regard, the Russian mathematician Aleksandr Lyapunov (1857–1918) and his asymptotic stability theory.

The main contribution of Poincaré to the present work is phase plane and stability analysis, as well as chaotic dynamics.

15. British School of Mathematics

1. Brook Taylor (1685–1731)
2. William Rowan Hamilton (1805–1865)
3. Sir George Stokes (1819–1903)

15.1   Brook Taylor (1685–1731)

Brook Taylor was an English mathematician who is best known for Taylor's theorem and the Taylor series. The Taylor Series can be used to represent a "smooth" function $f(x)$ as an infinite power series of terms expanded about a point $x = a$ using the functions derivatives of the form

$$f(x) = \sum_{n=0}^{\infty} \frac{f^{(n)}(a)}{n!} \left(x - a\right)^n.$$

Several other mathematicians, including James Gregory (1638–1675) and Colin Maclaurin (1698–1746) also worked in this area and published several results, but it was Brook Taylor who gave the general expression that now bears his name.

"How simple the Principles are, upon which the whole Art of Perspective depends."

The main contribution of Taylor to the present work is Taylor Series for function approximation.

15.2   William Rowan Hamilton (1805–1865)

William Hamilton was an Irish mathematician and physicist. He is best known for Hamiltonian mechanics and quaternions. Hamilton said of quaternions "Time is said to have only one dimension, and space to have three dimensions. . . . The mathematical quaternion partakes of both these elements; in technical language it may be said to be time plus space, or space plus time, and in this sense it has, or at least involves a reference to, four dimensions."

The main contribution of Hamilton is Hamiltonian dynamics, which is an alternative to Newton and Lagrangian dynamics.

"Who would not rather have the fame of Archimedes than that of his conqueror Marcellus?"

15.3   Sir George Stokes (1819–1903)

Stokes was a mathematician, physicist, politi-
cian and theologian. Stokes worked and studied at the University of Cambridge, and was
Lucasian Professor of Mathematics from 1849
until 1903. Stokes made seminal contributions
to fluid dynamics (including the Navier-Stokes
equations), optics, and mathematical physics
(including the first version of what is now
known as Stokes' theorem). He derived an
expression for the drag force exerted on spherical objects with small Reynolds numbers, as
well as terminal velocity studies. His work on
fluid motion and viscosity led to Stokes Law.
He published works on steady incompressible
fluids, wind and sound, friction of fluids in
motion and equilibrium and motion of elas-

*"Annihilation of work is no
less a physical impossibility
than its creation, that is,
than perpetual motion."*

tic solids. He is also known for his work on light, including studies of
polarization, aberration, diffraction, fluorescence and even chemical analysis. Stokes also studied railway accidents, and bridge engineering (civil
engineering).

The main contributions of Stokes to the present work are Stokes theorem, relating circulation and vorticity, and Navier-Stokes equations for
viscous flow.

16. Pioneers in Science and Engineering

1. Leonardo da Vinci (1452–1519), Italian
2. Nicolaus Copernicus (1473–1543), Polish
3. Galileo Galilei (1564–1642), Italian
4. Johannes Kepler (1571–1630), German
5. Konstantin Eduardovich Tsiolkovsky (1857–1935), Russian

16.1   Leonardo da Vinci (1452–1519)

During his lifetime Leonardo da Vinci was a celebrated engineer and artist, and today he is regarded as an early pioneer of flight science. Da Vinci is perhaps best known for his artistic legacy which includes such works as the *Mona Lisa*, *The Last Supper*, and the iconic *Vitruvian Man*. However, da Vinci was also a scientist and inventor with a keen grasp of mechanics and anatomy. Timoshenko actually refers to the genius and insight of da Vinci in his work *History of Strength of Materials*, pointing out that he made use of the method of moments and the principle of virtual displacements to analyze mechanical systems such as arches, pulleys, wire strength, scaffolds, and others. Timoshenko quotes da Vinci: "mechanics is the paradise of mathematical science because here we come to the fruits of mathematics." His studies were not only theoretical, but da Vinci also supported his ideas with many experiments. Several of da Vinci's detailed studies of anatomy, which included both humans and animals survive. One feature of da Vinci's studies is the visual representations accompanying his descriptions. Another is that he wrote in mirror script. In 1505 da Vinci produced a study on the flight of birds called *Codex on the Flight of Birds* and went on to make several conceptual drawings of flying machines, including a kind of rotary helicopter. Da Vinci was obsessed with flight remarking "when once you have tasted flight, you will forever walk the earth with your eyes turned skyward, for there you have been, and there you will always long to return." Most of da Vinci's surviving flying machines seem conceptually to function like a bird, or bat's wing. Da Vinci noted that for birds the center of pressure and center of mass are not the same, thereby making an essential discovery regarding static stability in flight. In this work da Vinci also made numerous remarks about the use of control surfaces in flight, including parachutes.

"Simplicity is the ultimate sophistication."

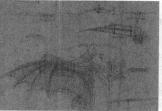

Figure 91: Helicopter (*left*), detailed armature for a wing (*middle*), a machine that flies by flapping wings (*right*).

The main contribution of Leonardo da Vinci to the present work is the law of conservation of mass in channels, and his work pioneering work on fluid mechanics and aerodynamics.

16.2 Nicolaus Copernicus (1473–1543)

While it was Aristarchus of Samos (310–230 BCE) who first postulated that the Earth goes around the fixed Sun in a circular orbit, it was Copernicus who first gave evidence for this idea. Copernicus was a polyglot, polymath and lawyer. Copernicus's famous 1543 work *De revolutionibus orbium coelestium* effectively ended the geocentric idea that had dominated since Ptolemy (90–168 CE) published his *Almagest*. It is for this reason that Copernicus is often considered a "father of modern astronomy," a title he shares with Galileo Galilei. It is argued that many other contributors played a small role in this paradigm shift, or had proposed corrections to Ptolemy's work, nevertheless, no one else before Copernicus was so clear with the statement of the Heliocentric Theory. Copernicus observed that the Earth rotated around its axis and all the planets orbited

"The massive bulk of the earth does indeed shrink to insignificance in comparison with the size of the heavens."

around the sun without the aid of a telescope, which would be invented later by Galileo. Copernicus is also regarded for discovering a principle in economics, sometimes called Gresham's Law, but also called Copernicus's Law, which explains how competing types of money with different values will flow in and out of circulation when controlled by a government. This idea and other notable economic ideas were published by Copernicus in *Monetae cudendae ratio* in 1526.

The main contribution of Copernicus to the present work is his revolutionary ideas about a heliocentric system.

16.3   Galileo Galilei (1564–1642)

Galileo Galilei was a brilliant and bold astronomer, engineer and physicist that contributed so much to the advancement of science that he is sometimes called "the father of modern science." Not only did he make many notable discoveries with his telescope, during the course of his life, but he also made several brave stands against the church that could have easily resulted in his execution or imprisonment. Galileo had a penetrating insight and perspective, which is evident in his remark "the Milky Way is nothing else but a mass of innumerable stars planted together in clusters." In his fight with the church, the

Galileo Galilei.

"If I were again beginning my studies, I would follow the advice of Plato and start with mathematics."

church essentially made their case on the basis of several bible passages, all of which basically contain the phrase "the world is established; it shall never be moved." Galileo tempted fate by asserting "I do not feel obliged to believe that the same God who has endowed us with sense, reason, and intellect has intended us to forgo their use" and "it vexes me when they would constrain science by the authority of the Scriptures, and yet do not consider themselves bound to answer reason and experiment."

Each time Galileo was called to testify for his crimes against the Catholic church, he simply did as he was told to do, and lied in such tremendously over-the-top fashion to the church inquisitors about how sorry he was for his crimes, it is actually quite humorous to read the dialogues. Galileo simply had no intention, nor felt any need, to be a martyr for his discoveries. Obviously the truth and genius of Galileo has since been shown and the church has several times issued apologies for, and analysis of, the events. In *Starry Messenger*, Galileo published his observations about the moon's craters, that he could see many times more stars through his telescope than the naked eye, and that Jupiter had moons orbiting it. From the observation of Jupiter's orbiting moons, Galileo correctly concluded that not everything orbits Earth. Galileo was also the first to notice that falling bodies due to gravity have velocity and acceleration independent of mass, contrary to Aristotle's dogma. Galileo made many other astronomical discoveries, including the rings of Saturn, the phases of Venus, Sun spots and others. In his work "Two new sciences" Galileo also made contributions to material science by studying fracture mechanics in the context of cantilever beams. Galileo also invented the thermometer.

The main contributions of Galileo to the present work are his first law of motion (in the absence of force, the velocity of mass will remain constant), and that projectiles in constant gravity follow parabolic trajectories. After all, he is considered the father of modern science!

16.4   Johannes Kepler (1571–1630)

Johannes Kepler was a mathematician and astronomer, that is best known for his laws of planetary motion. Kepler notes that the radius vector sweeps equal areas in equal times, and the Earth moves in ellipses with the Sun at one focus. Kepler's work was essential for development of the laws of universal gravitation, and ultimately the groundbreaking and comprehensive theory set forth by Newton in *Principia*.

In orbital mechanics, Kepler's equation

$$M = E - \epsilon \sin(E)$$

is a relationship between M, the time to reach certain angle, E is the eccentric anomaly, and ϵ, the eccentricity of a given orbit. This equa-

"I much prefer the sharpest criticism of a single intelligent man to the thoughtless approval of the masses."

tion applies to orbits which are conic sections: circle, ellipse, parabola, or hyperbola, and will occur in a two dimensional orbital plane.

For an elliptic, parabolic, or hyperbolic orbit (the Keplerian orbits), the following vis-à-vis equation holds

$$v^2 = \mu \left(\frac{2}{r} - \frac{1}{a} \right)$$

where $\mu = GM$, G is the universal gravitational constant, M is the mass of the star, and a is the semi-major axis of the orbit, v is the relative speed of the two bodies, and r is the distance between them.

The main contributions of Kepler to the present work are his three conjectures for planetary motion, as well as his equation for determining orbital motion.

16.5   Konstantin Eduardovich Tsiolkovsky (1857–1935)

Tsiolkovsky was a pioneer of rocket science. He shares the title "Father of Rocket Science" with German scientist Hermann Oberth (1894–1989) and the American Robert H. Goddard (1882–1945). He is probably best known for Tsiolkovsky's Rocket Equation, which is given by

$$\Delta v = v_e \ln \left(\frac{m_i}{m_f} \right).$$

In this equation, the change in velocity (Δv) for a rocket is given as a function of the propellant's relative exhaust velocity (v_e), and the initial (m_i), and final (m_f) mass of the rocket.

"All the Universe is full of the life of perfect creatures."

The above relation is the solution of the Tsiolkovsky equation given by

$$m \frac{dv}{dt} = F$$

where $F = v_e dm/dt$. The Tsiolkovsky Equation accounts for the change in velocity due to change in mass. A rocket prior to launch is mostly fuel. As the fuel burns the rocket's velocity increases. As more fuel burns the rocket loses mass, and the velocity further increases.

Tsiolkovsky wrote more than 400 works, including approximately 90 published works specifically about rockets and space travel. Much of Tsiolkovsky's writings were philosophical and creative investigations, but did have many practical ideas and an excellent knowledge of biology, physics and mathematics. He theorized vectorizable thrusters, multistage rockets, space stations, airlocks, and atmosphere systems. He built Russia's first wind tunnel and his work is thought to have had a strong contribution to the success of the Soviet space program. Tsiolkovsky also did other original work on airships, airplanes, trains, and hovercraft. His idea for an all metal dirigible airship, called *Aerostat Metallitscheski* was published in 1892. Most of his ideas were considered impractical and science fiction at that time. Tsiolkovsky was undoubtedly a creative pioneer who had several prescient ideas about the future of mankind in space, as well as practical investigations of the associated physical principles.

The main contributions of Tsiolkovsky to the present work are his description of the motion of rockets in space in terms of the rate of discharge of mass, and also the idea of multi-stage rockets. He is considered the father of rocketry in Russia.

17. Structures and Vibrations

1. Robert Hooke FRS (1635–1703), English
2. John William Strutt, 3rd Baron Rayleigh (1842–1919), English

17.1   Robert Hooke (1635–1703)

Robert Hooke was a talented and prolific natural philosopher and polymath. He was a great creative thinker who studied and had scientifically correct ideas in many areas, but a weakness of his is that he rarely carried his investigations far enough to be the person that history remembers. Despite his numerous ideas and achievements, this issue may have contributed to his relative historical obscurity in consideration of his profound contributions. Hooke is remembered for his spring law

$$F = -kx$$

"The Reason of making Experiments is, for the Discovery of the Method of Nature, in its Progress and Operations."

which is particularly useful for describing the deformation of an elastic
body with a restoring force. Hooke is to be greatly credited for his work in
material science leading up to the idea that a deformation (essentially the
strain) produced is proportional to the magnitude of an applied force. Hooke
reached this conclusion by numerous experiments with weights applied to
various materials, such as strings, springs and even wooden beams, not-
ing that the deformation was approximately linearly proportional to the
weight. The modern theory of elasticity, essentially built on Hooke's law,
says that the strain of an elastic object is proportional to the stress applied
to it.

An example of Hooke's great contribution follows from a 1670 lecture
delivered at the Royal Society where he was the first to give a version of
what is now called Newton's three laws of motion. Hooke explained

1. First, that all Celestial Bodies whatsoever, have an attraction or gravi-
   tating power towards their own Centers.
2. Second, that all bodies whatsoever that are put into a direct and simple
   motion, will continue to move forward in a straight line.
3. Third, that these attractive powers are so much the more powerful in
   operating, by how much the nearer the body brought upon to their own
   centers.

He went on to say "I have not yet experimentally verified . . . a certain rule,"
referring to the inverse square law, and this is exactly where Isaac Newton
later succeeded with a precise statement of the universal law of gravitation and demonstration of that fact. Newton later acknowledged in *Principia* that it was a series of correspondence with Hooke that rekindled
his interest in studying astronomical laws. Some of Hooke's other notable
achievements were in timekeeping and finding longitude at sea, in biology
and coining of the word "cell," paleontology, a model of human memory,
architecture (he helped rebuild London after the great fire of 1666), and
astronomy.

The main contribution of Hooke to the present work is Hooke's spring
law ($F = -kx$).

17.2 John William Strutt, 3rd Baron Rayleigh (1842–1919)

Rayleigh was an English physicist who is probably best known for his discovery of the essentially inert noble gas element argon, which is third most abundant in Earth's air. That work was jointly carried out with Sir William Ramsay (1862–1916), and Rayleigh won the 1904 Nobel Prize in Physics for the discovery. Rayleigh is also known for Rayleigh scattering and Rayleigh waves. Rayleigh wrote a still popular textbook called *The Theory of Sound*. Rayleigh is well known for his work on dimensional analysis, and the Buckingham-π Theorem is just a generalization of Rayleigh's method. The importance of dimensional analysis is that one can determine the dimensional parameters for a given set of variables, even without knowing the governing equations. In fluid mechanics, Rayleigh is especially well known for Rayleigh-Bénard convection and the Rayleigh-Taylor instability. There is also a dimensionless Rayleigh number that typically

"A young author who believes himself capable of great things would usually do well to secure the favourable recognition of the scientific world by work whose scope is limited, and whose value is easily judged, before embarking upon higher flights."

shows up in buoyancy driven flows and is the product of the Grashof number and Prandtl number. Rayleigh also did work on shock waves. Rayleigh discovered the importance of viscosity to shock structure, which added to the understanding of conduction's importance to shock structure discovered by Rankine. The Rayleigh–Ritz method, named after Rayleigh and Walther Ritz (1878–1909), is a useful and popular algorithm for computing eigenvalues and eigenvectors for a linear system.

The main contributions of Rayleigh to the present work are his book on *The Theory of Sound* and his non-dimensional analysis.

18. Fluid and Aerodynamics

1. Heinrich Gustav Magnus (1802–1870), German
2. Nikolay Yegorovich Zhukovsky (1847–1921), Russian
3. Ludwig Prandtl (1875–1953), German
4. Ernst Mach (1838–1916), Austrian
5. Osborne Reynolds (1842–1912), Irish/English
6. Claude Louis Marie Henri Navier (1785–1836), French
7. Gustaf de Laval (1845–1913), Swedish

18.1 Heinrich Gustav Magnus (1802–1870)

Magnus was a prolific researcher and experimentalist. Magnus is best known for the Magnus Effect which describes the normal force of
a rotating cylinder in a stream of gas.

Magnus main contribution to the present
work is his pioneering studies of lift in modern
aerodynamics.

18.2 Nikolay Yegorovich Zhukovsky (1847–1921)

Zhukovsky, also commonly spelled Joukowsky,
was a Russian mathematician and engineer,
and is considered the father of aerodynamics
in Russia. He is especially well-known for the
Zhukovsky Transformation, which is given by

$$X = x \left(1 + \frac{b^2}{x^2 + y^2} \right)$$

$$Y = y \left(1 - \frac{b^2}{x^2 + y^2} \right)$$

$$a^2 = (b - \epsilon)^2 + \mu^2.$$

This relation maps a circle of radius a, with center (μ, ϵ) into a Zhukovsky Airfoil. Kutta-Joukowski theorem, named also after German mathematician Martin Wilhelm Kutta (1867–1944), states that lift is proportional to circulation, where circulation is defined as the integral of the tangential velocity to a closed circuit enclosing the airfoil.

Joukowsky also played an important role in the development of rotor aerodynamics, especially the theory of momentum, including torque and angular momentum, as well as vorticity. Starting in 1912 with the publication of "Vortex theory of screw propeller," Joukowsky pioneered this field.

The main contribution of Zhukovsky to the present work his lift theorem.

18.3 Ludwig Prandtl (1875–1953)

Prandtl was a German engineer known for extensive contributions to aerodynamics. Prandtl was not only a pioneer in the field, but taught many students that went on to become distinguished leaders such as: Ackeret, Blasius, Busemann, Munk, Schlichting, Tietjens, von Karman, Meyer, and many others (over 80 students). Consequently Prandtl had a far reaching legacy on aerodynamics. Prandtl introduced the concept of boundary layers and the lifting line theory (and vortex drag), which is essential for aeroplane design. Prandtl also pioneered studies in subsonic and supersonic aerodynamics. Prandtl was elected to be a fellow of the Royal Society in 1928.

The main contributions of Prandtl to the present work are boundary layers for high Reynold's number flow, compressible flows, and he is considered the father of modern aerodynamics.

Prandtl's work stands out due to the combination of his specialist knowledge and his grasp of mathematics, a marked intuitive ability and the originality of his thought. At the same time, he also has a great interest in education.

18.4   Ernst Mach (1838–1916)

Mach was a physicist, psychologist, and philosopher best known for his research on shock waves, and in particular for Mach number. For his work in philosophy, Mach is considered a "father of the philosophy of science." Mach received a PhD in physics from the University of Vienna in 1860. In 1864 he became Professor of Mathematics at the University of Graz, and later Professor of Physics at the Charles University in Prague where he would remain for nearly 30 years until eventually returning to the University of Vienna. Mach is best known for his works *The Science of Mechanics* (1883), *The Analysis of Sensations* (1897), *Popular Scientific Lectures* (1895), *The Principles of Physical Optics* (1913), *Knowledge and Error* (1905), and *Principles of the Theory of Heat* (1896). In 1877 Mach published the key work leading to a theory of sound effects observed during supersonic motion. Mach experimentally found evidence for shocks as well. The ratio of the speed of projectile to the speed of sound v_p/v_s is now called the Mach number, M_a.

The main contribution of Mach to the present work is supersonic flows and the Mach number.

"The student of mathematics often finds it hard to throw off the uncomfortable feeling that his science, in the person of his pencil, surpasses him in intelligence,-an impression which the great Euler confessed he often could not get rid of. This feeling finds a sort of justification when we reflect that the majority of the ideas we deal with were conceived by others, often centuries ago. In a great measure it is really the intelligence of other people that confronts us in science."

18.5 Osborne Reynolds (1842–1912)

Reynolds is best known for Reynolds number, a term that was introduced by Arnold Sommerfeld (1868–1951) while presenting a paper in 1908 on hydrodynamic stability that involved what is today called the Orr-Sommerfeld equation. The Orr-Sommerfeld equation, also named after William McFadden Orr (1866–1934) is derived from a perturbation of the Navier Stokes equations and contains the Reynolds number. In 1893 Reynolds published "An experimental investigation of the circumstances which determine whether the motion of water shall be direct or sinuous, and of the law of resistance in parallel channels," and in 1895 Reynolds published "On the dynamical theory of incompressible viscous fluids and the determination of the criterion." These two works were pioneering studies on transition from laminar to turbulent flow. He also introduced the modern form

"[To] mechanical progress there is apparently no end: for as in the past so in the future, each step in any direction will remove limits and bring in past barriers which have till then blocked the way in other directions; and so what for the time may appear to be a visible or practical limit will turn out to be but a bend in the road."

$$Re = \frac{\rho U D}{\mu} = \frac{U D}{\nu}.$$

The dimensionless Reynolds number is the ratio of inertial forces to viscous forces. Reynolds also proposed what is now known as Reynolds-averaging of turbulent flows, where quantities such as velocity are expressed as the sum of mean and fluctuating components. Such averaging allows for 'bulk' description of turbulent flow, for example using the Reynolds-averaged Navier Stokes equations.

The main contribution of Reynolds to the present work is his work on viscous flow in channels and Reynolds number.

18.6   Claude Louis Marie Henri Navier (1785–1836)

Navier was a French engineer, sometimes considered the father of structural analysis. He was famous in his time for pioneering work on suspension bridges. Later in life, he also gained considerable prestige for his contributions to France as a civil engineer advising on the construction of roads and railways, as well as on how technology and science could be used to improve life. Today, Navier is best known for the Navier Stokes equations which describe fluid flow. This is the same as the Euler equations, except now with the addition of the viscous terms. The idea of no-slip boundary condition was also pioneered by Navier, which states that there is no relative velocity between a particle of fluid and the adjacent solid surface. Navier correctly described this system for an incompressible flow in 1821 and for a compressible flow in 1822. Navier is also known for his contribution to the theory of elasticity and strength of materials. He also defined the elastic modulus. In 1824 Navier was elected to the Académie des Sciences.

The main contributions of Navier to the present work is his Navier-Stokes equations for viscous flow.

18.7   Gustaf de Laval (1845–1913)

Gustaf de Laval was a Swedish engineer that is best known for his design of the converging-diverging nozzle that is used in rocket engines, but originally Laval used this nozzle to design an efficient single-stage steam turbine. Laval's steam turbine design is still in use today! The goal of the steam turbine engine was to efficiently power a generator that could rotate conductors through a magnetic field in order to make electricity. In order to make the turbine spin fast, which is essential for making power, the Laval nozzle converts the very high pressure at the inlet of the nozzle into high velocity at the outlet, which in turns spins the turbine through attached fan blades. The converging part of the nozzle accelerates subsonic flow by decreasing pressure and temperature, the diverging part accelerates supersonic flow by further decreasing the pressure and temperature, and at design conditions, the throat is sonic. Laval originally invented the nozzle in 1888 for use with steam turbine engines. Steam turbine engines remained the Laval nozzle's primary application until Robert Hutchings Goddard (1882–1945) pioneered their use in rockets, finding they resulted in tremendously increased efficiency. Laval also invented a submarine and was known for his agricultural inventions, such as a centrifugal cream separator. In fact, Laval founded a company in 1883 called Alfa Laval that is still in business today!

The main contribution of de Laval to the present work is his convergent divergent nozzle which was essential for rockets to escape the gravity of Earth (under design conditions where the throat is sonic, and the mass flow rate per unit area is maximum, and the exit velocity is supersonic after the expansion in the divergent part).

19. Thermodynamics and Heat Transfer

1. James Prescott Joule (1818–1889), English
2. Hermann Ludwig Ferdinand von Helmholtz (1821–1894), German
3. Nicolas Léonard Sadi Carnot (1796–1832), French
4. Rudolf Clausius (1822–1888), German
5. William Thomson, 1st Baron Kelvin (1824–1907), British
6. Ludwig Eduard Boltzmann (1844–1906), Austrian
7. Josiah Willard Gibbs (1839–1903), American

19.1   James Prescott Joule (1818–1889)

William Thomson (Kelvin) wrote of Joule that "[He] fully established the relations of equivalence among the energies of chemical affinity, of heat, of combination or combustion, of electrical currents in the galvanic battery, of electrical currents in magnetoelectric machines, of engines worked by galvanism, and of all the varied and interchangeable manifestations of calorific action and mechanical force which accompany them. These researches, with the theory of animal heat and motion in relation to the heat of combustion of the food, and the theory of the phenomena presented by shooting stars, due to the same penetrating investigator, have afforded to the author of the present communication the chief groundwork for his speculations." Joule was a physicist that

"My object has been, first to discover correct principles and then to suggest their practical development."

had far reaching impact on thermodynamics, and revolutionized the landscape by, with great difficulty and effort, overturning the Caloric Theory of Heat, put forth by the revered Lavoisier and Carnot, and supported by most other academics at the time. Not only is Joule credited with the first law of thermodynamics, by discovering the relationship between heat and mechanical work, he also discovered the relationship between heat and current passing through a conductor. The later is explained by Joule's Law which states that the heat release is proportional to the product of the current squared, the resistance and the time

$$H \propto I^2 \cdot R \cdot t$$

The SI energy unit is named Joule in his honor. Joule also worked with Kelvin on the absolute temperature scale.

The main contribution of Joule to the present work is the first law of thermodynamics.

19.2 Hermann Ludwig Ferdinand von Helmholtz (1821–1894)

Helmholtz was a German mathematician, physicist, physician and engineer, that is especially known for his work on thermodynamics, especially conservation of energy. James Clerk Maxwell wrote of Helmholtz's effect on the field "To appreciate the full scientific value of Helmholtz's little essay on this subject we should have to ask those to whom we owe the greatest discoveries in thermodynamics and other branches of modern physics, how many times they have read it over, and how often during their researches they felt the weighty statements of Helmholtz acting on their minds like an irresistible driving-power." Helmholtz's first physics paper from 1847, "On the Conservation of Force" was actually a paper intended

"Whoever, in the pursuit of science, seeks after immediate practical utility may rest assured that he seeks in vain."

for medical doctors in an attempt to discover what physical laws were necessary for perpetual motion by matter of examining the laws of nature. The work was seen as speculative and a highly theoretical waste of time by most, but some, like Carl Gustav Jacob Jacobi (1804–1851) recognized its significance. Helmholtz developed several important theorems about vorticity called Helmholtz First, Second and Third Theorems. The most important is the third theorem which states that a flow that is initially vorticity free will remain vorticity free. The three theorems were a precursor to Kelvin's circulation theorem. Also he is known for Helmholtz condition, Helmholtz decomposition, Helmholtz equation, Helmholtz free energy, Helmholtz free entropy, Kelvin-Helmholtz instability, Kelvin-Helmholtz mechanism, Hydrodynamic stability, Keratometer, and Supercapacitor.

The main contribution of Helmholtz to the present work is the law of the conservation of total energy.

19.3   Nicolas Léonard Sadi Carnot (1796–1832)

Carnot was French soldier and physicist who did pioneering work in thermodynamics. Carnot is sometimes called "the father of thermodynamics," but this title is rightly shared with several other major contributors including Joule, von Helmholtz, Clausius, Kelvin, Gibbs, and Boltzmann. Carnot is best known for his work on what is now called: Carnot cycle, Carnot efficiency, Carnot theorem, and Carnot heat engine. Carnot's major published work was "Reflections on the Motive Power of Fire." Carnot also developed a theory of the heat engine. Carnot died at just 36 because of cholera.

"The production of motive power is therefore due in steam engines not to actual consumption of caloric but to its transportation from a warm body to a cold body."

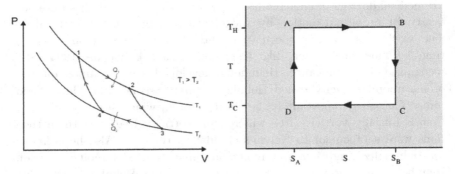

Figure 92:   Carnot cycles for heat engine: Pressure/Volume (PV) diagram (*left*) and Temperature/Entropy (TS) diagram (*right*).

    The main contribution of Carnot to the present work is Carnot Cycle of thermodynamics.

19.4 Rudolf Clausius (1822–1888)

Clausius was a mathematician and physicist that did pioneering work in thermodynamics. His most famous works study the mechanical properties of heat, and entropy. Clausius stated in 1865, that "the energy of the universe is constant," and "the entropy of the universe tends to a maximum," effectively giving the first and second law of thermodynamics. One of Clausius's most important works "On the Moving Force of Heat," develops the idea of the first and second laws of thermodynamics. Clausius introduced the concept of entropy and was the first to give it a mathematical basis. Clausius also fixed the Caloric Theory of Combustion by replacing conservation of heat with conservation of energy, which was important for the development of the modern theory of thermodynamics.

"Heat can never pass from a colder to a warmer body without some other change connected therewith, occurring at the same time."

The main contributions of Clausius to the present work are the second law of thermodynamics, as well as his work on entropy.

19.5 William Thomson, 1st Baron Kelvin (1824–1907)

Kelvin was a mathematician, physicist and engineer who is especially known for his contributions to thermodynamics. Absolute temperatures are stated in units of Kelvin in his honor. While the existence of a lower limit to temperature (absolute zero) was known prior to his work, Lord Kelvin is widely known for determining its correct value as approximately -273.15 degree Celsius or -459.67 degree Fahrenheit. He was the first British scientist to be admitted to the House of Lords, becoming Baron Kelvin for his work on Thermodynamics. Also working on flight science, Kelvin's circulation theorem states that the

"Bring forward what is true, Write it so that it is clear, Defend it to your last breath!"

circulation around a closed contour with conservative body forces is constant for an ideal fluid whose density only depends on pressure. Kelvin is also known for Kelvin transform, Kelvin–Helmholtz instability, Kelvin–Helmholtz mechanism, and Kelvin–Helmholtz luminosity.

The main contributions of Kelvin to the present work are his formulation (with Max Planck) of the second law of thermodynamics and his work on temperature scale.

19.6   Ludwig Eduard Boltzmann (1844–1906)

Boltzmann was an Austrian physicist who pioneered the study of statistical mechanics. Boltzmann's work was instrumental for the development of the modern kinetic theory of gases. At the time, many prominent scientists rejected the idea of the atomic and molecular structure of gases and matter at the microscale. Boltzmann's work was important for modernizing the second law of thermodynamics with a probabilistic model of microscale collisions maximizing entropy. Boltmann's entropy formula is given by

$$S = k \log W$$

"Let us have free scope for all directions of research; away with dogmatism, either atomistic or anti-atomistic!"

and relates the entropy to a statistical number of states (in this case, molecular configurations of a gas) which is proportional to W. The famous formula is carved on his gravestone. Boltzmann in 1872 was the first to give the correct statistical (thermodynamic) entropy function for the case of an ideal gas.

The main contributions of Boltzmann to the present work are his work on heat radiation and the statistical interpretation of entropy.

19.7   Josiah Willard Gibbs (1839–1903)

Gibbs was a physicist, chemist and mathematician, who made contributions to the theoretical foundations of thermodynamics and
statistical mechanics. Along with Maxwell and
Botlzmann, Gibbs is one of the "fathers of
statistical mechanics," a field whose name he
invented. Gibb's explained thermodynamics in
terms of particles in such a way that Poincaré
wrote of his ideas "Let a drop of wine fall into
a glass of water; whatever be the law that gov-
erns the internal movement of the liquid, we
will soon see it tint itself uniformly pink and
from that moment on, however we may agitate
the vessel, it appears that the wine and water
can separate no more. All this, Maxwell and
Boltzmann have explained, but the one who
saw it in the cleanest way, in a book that is

*"One of the principal
objects of theoretical research is to find the point
of view from which the subject appears in the greatest
simplicity."*

too little read because it is difficult to read, is Gibbs, in his Principles of
Statistical Mechanics." That is high praise from Poincaré and suggests that
Gibbs's work is overlooked for its difficulty despite its high quality. His work
on the applications of thermodynamics was instrumental in transforming
physical chemistry into a rigorous deductive science. Gibbs also worked on
the application of Maxwell's equations to problems in physical optics, and
made contributions to vector calculus.

The main contribution of Gibbs to the present work is his work on
thermodynamics of chemical reactions.

20. Chemistry and Combustion

1. Antoine-Laurent de Lavoisier (1743–1794), French
2. Svante Arrhenius (1859–1927), Swedish

20.1   Antoine-Laurent de Lavoisier (1743–1794)

Antoine-Laurent de Lavoisier was a French chemist that contributed so much to the science he is sometimes regarded as "father of modern chemistry." Lavoisier is particularly regarded for being an experimentalist and being one of the first chemists to employ the scientific method. Lavoisier is probably most famous for discovering the essential effect of oxygen during combustion processes. This work and the experiments that Lavoisier designed to prove the idea lead to the end of Johann Becher's (1635–1682) popular, but wrong, Phlogiston Theory of combustion which hypothesized the existence of a fictional fire-element called Phlogiston contained in all combustible materials. Lavoisier was one of the first chemists to study stoichiometry and consider quantitatively the elemental form of chemical reactions by conservation of atoms. For example, hydrogen and oxygen can be combined to produce water

"We must trust to nothing but facts: These are presented to us by Nature, and cannot deceive. We ought, in every instance, to submit our reasoning to the test of experiment, and never to search for truth but by the natural road of experiment and observation."

$$2H_2 + O_2 \rightleftharpoons 2H_2O + \text{heat}.$$

Lavoisier was also a pioneer in modernizing the understanding and labeling of chemical elements. His work published in 1787, *Method of Chemical Nomenclature*, outlined the modern program. The primitive idea dating back to the Greek's notion from the Platonic solids of, for example, "Earth" and "Air" was replaced by essentially our modern idea of the chemical elements. Lavoisier's work, which included some 33 elements organized into metals, nonmetals, earths, and gases, was a giant leap in progress toward the modern periodic table. In 1789, Lavoisier published his *Elementary Treatise on Chemistry* which summarized his and other known chemistry into a single authoritative work.

Lavoisier also advanced knowledge of how respiration works by relating the process to combustion. During the French Revolution (1789–1799) Lavoisier was executed by beheading in 1794 during Maximilien Robespierre's (1758–1794) "reign of terror" convicted of having been a tax-collector. At the time he was also an extraordinarily successful Royal Arsenal chemist for the then immensely unpopular Ferme générale, of the Ancien Régime, that greatly improved France's gunpowder. His friend Lagrange wrote of the act "It took them only an instant to cut off that head, but France may not produce another like it in a century." In an odd twist of fate, his accuser Robespierre, was executed just 2 months later during the upheaval, partly for his reckless execution of others.

The main contributions of Lavoisier to the present work are the law of conservation of the number of atoms and he is considered the father of modern chemistry.

20.2 Svante Arrhenius (1859–1927)

Svante Arrhenius was a Swedish scientist and Nobel Prize winner in chemistry (1903) for his "electrolytic theory of dissociation." Arrhenius is regarded as one of the fathers of physical chemistry and is perhaps best known for his 1896 work describing the Greenhouse Effect giving a quantitative relationship between carbon dioxide (CO_2) levels in the atmosphere and surface temperature of the Earth. The Arrhenius Equation which relates equilibrium rate constants to heat of reaction

$$\Omega = De^{-\frac{E_a}{RT}}$$

"Humanity stands... before a great problem of finding new raw materials and new sources of energy."

is a law describing chemical heat release. Arrhenius noted that this equation followed from the earlier work of Jacobus Henricus van't Hoff (1852–1911), and what is called the van't Hoff Equation which relates equilibrium constants of a chemical reaction to the enthalpy and temperature.

The Arrhenius states the rate constant of a chemical reaction Ω equals the product of a pre-exponential collision frequency factor D and an exponential function of E_a the activation energy, R the gas constant, and temperature T. D is related to what is called the Dahmkoler number and is typically the ratio of the characteristic fluid time over the characteristic chemical reaction time. D and E_a are typically experimentally determined. The Arrhenius law is designed to limit the reacting molecules to those that have a certain minimum amount of energy, an energy of activation E_a. Increasing temperature increases the reaction rate slowly until a critical temperature range is reached, and then temperature increases rapidly. The Arrhenius law is associated with periods of latency, or slow changes then fast changes, and therefore can contribute to making a system of governing equations stiff, in particular, when fluid mechanics is considered, as well as the ratio of fluid and chemical time scales, needs to be taken into account.

The main contribution of Arrhenius to the present work is his formula for the energy released by chemical reactions.

21. Electricity and Magnetism

1. Charles-Augustin de Coulomb (1736–1806)
2. Gustav Robert Kirchhoff (1824–1887)
3. James Clerk Maxwell (1831–1879)

21.1 Charles-Augustin de Coulomb (1736–1806)

Coulomb began his career as an officer in the Royal Engineer Corps. Coulomb was a French physicist best known for Coulomb's Law for the electrostatic force F_e, which is given by

$$F_e = \frac{kq_1q_2}{r^2}$$

where q_1 and q_2 are charges, r is the distance between them and $k = 8.99 \cdot 10^9 \, \mathrm{Nm^2/C^2}$ is the electrostatic constant. Coulomb's Law states that like charges attract and opposite charges repel, with a force proportional to the inverse square of the distance between them. Coulomb is also known for studying friction between solids. Coulomb performed experiments that were important for the development of this law, and were fundamental for the theory of electrostatics. Around 1777 Coulomb devel-

"...the repulsive action which the two balls exert on each other when they are electrified similarly is in the inverse ratio of the square of the distances."

oped a technique using a device he invented called a Torsion Balance to measure electrostatic forces. Torsion balances proved useful to calculate weak forces, and were also later used to calculate the gravitational constant (for example by Henry Cavendish (1731–1810) in what is called the Cavendish Experiment from 1798). After his death his work continued to gain acceptance and traction, and his researches were continued by many eminent scholars, especially Jean-Baptiste Biot (1774–1862).

The main contribution of Coulomb to the present work is Coulomb's Law, and Coulombs (C), the SI unit of charge named after him.

21.2   Gustav Robert Kirchhoff (1824–1887)

Kirchhoff was a German physicist best known for his work on electrical circuits. Kirchhoff made major contributions, and is especially known for what is called Kirchhoff's voltage law which can be stated as: the sum of the products of the resistances of conductors and the current in them around a closed loop is equal to the total electromotive force present in the loop. There is also a Kirchhoff's law for current. Kirchhoff is also known for other important contributions to physics such as mass spectroscopy.

"Look here, I have succeeded at last in fetching some gold from the sun."

The main contributions of Kirchhoff to the present work are his voltage and current laws.

21.3   James Clerk Maxwell (1831–1879)

Maxwell was a Scottish physicist known mostly for his extensive and important contributions to electricity and magnetism. In this area, Maxwell's work is considered fundamental and represents one of the most important theoretical developments in physics ever achieved, side-by-side with Newton and Einstein's work. Maxwell is also well known for his contributions to thermodynamics, the kinetic theory of gases, control theory, and even color vision, perception and photography. It is perhaps lesser known, but quite interesting to note that Maxwell's technique was used in the production of the first color photograph.

"It is of great advantage to the student of any subject to read the original memoirs on that subject, for science is always most completely assimilated when it is in the nascent state."

The main contribution of Maxwell to the present work is his pioneering studies on heat as a form of energy.

PART IV

Miscellanea

22. Summary, Final Remarks and Takeaways

The following few pages will help the reader to review the main concepts and techniques discussed in this book and put them in perspective.

22.1 Basic Mathematics: Geometry, Algebra and Calculus

The Fundamental Theorem of Geometry, due to Pythagoras, defines the distance between two points in two and three dimensions. The equation of a line and a plane in Cartesian coordinates are given as well as the equations of circles and other conic sections. Trigonometry is used throughout the book. The Fundamental Theorem of Algebra, due to Gauss, gives the number of roots of a polynomial counting multiplicity. Gaussian Elimination for linear algebraic equations is discussed with two examples, the intersection of two lines, and three planes. Also Cramer's Rule is used to determine whether there is no solution, one solution, or multiple solutions for a system of equations. Nonlinear scalar and systems of equations are solved, with Kepler's equation and Global Positioning System (GPS) as examples. Applications of Newton's Method to the equation

$$z^4 = 1,$$

using complex numbers is chosen to introduce fractals.

While Algebra deals with operations on numbers, Calculus deals with operations on functions. In fact, Calculus is the study of change; the rate of change is the derivative of a function and the accumulation or summation of incremental changes yields the total change of the function. The Fundamental Theorem of Calculus, due to Newton, plays an important role in the book: integration annihilates differentiation (and vice-versa), hence the integral of the derivative of the function, gives back the function plus a constant of integration.

We start with polynomial functions and find their derivatives. Geometrically the derivative is the slope of the tangent of the function at a point. It can be obtained as the limit of the slope of a chord in the close neighborhood of a point. The integral is obtained via the concept of antiderivative based on the Fundamental Theorem of Calculus. This theorem is used also to solve differential equations:

$$\frac{df}{dt} = g(f, t).$$

Integrating both sides gives

$$\int_{t_0}^{t} \frac{df}{dt} d\tau = \int_{t_0}^{t} g(f, \tau) d\tau = f(t) - f(t_0),$$

where $f(t_0)$ is the constant of integration. There are two obvious special cases, if g is a function of t only, or if g is a function of f only. In the first case, the differential equation is solved by simple integration, while in the second case we have a separable differential equation, which can also be solved by integration

$$\int \frac{df}{g(f)} = \int dt$$

to obtain t as a function of f, namely the inverse function of f.

Calculus is a two-way street. If $f(t)$ is given, we can find df/dt by differentiation. Repeating the process we find the second derivative, which is the derivative of the derivative

$$\frac{d}{dt} \left(\frac{df}{dt} \right) = \frac{d^2 f}{dt^2}.$$

For example, if $f(t)$ is the distance covered at time t, the first derivative, df/dt, is the speed, and the second derivative, $d^2 f/dt^2$, is the acceleration. Obviously we need the second derivative to study Newton's second law of motion

$$F = m \cdot a.$$

If the independent (running) variable is replaced by x, the coordinate in space, $f(x)$ now represents the shape of the curve, while the derivative is the slope of the tangent to the curve at any point x, and the second derivative, assuming the curve is shallow (namely $|df/dx| \ll 1$), is approximately the curvature. Here, the curvature is approximated by the rate of change of the slope of the tangent. We need the second derivative to study bending and buckling since in these problems the moment is proportional to curvature.

On the other hand, if the acceleration (the curvature) is given, we can find the speed (or the slope of the tangent), by integrating once. By integrating again, we find the function itself, depending on t (or x). Notice the second route is producing a solution to a differential equation which is a relation between the function and its derivatives. However, every integration process produces a constant of integration, and to fix the solution we should impose a condition to determine that constant.

Next, if the function and its derivatives are known at a point, one can construct an approximation of this function in a neighborhood of this point in terms of a polynomial, where the coefficients of the terms are given by the derivatives of the function. This polynomial is the first few terms of the Taylor Series expansion of the function. There are many applications of this polynomial. For example, in Newton's Method to solve nonlinear equations, a linear approximation involving the first derivative is used. While, approximation including the second derivative is needed in optimization problems, to find where the function is locally minimum or maximum.

22.2   Elementary Functions and Their Differential Equations

There are four elementary functions heavily used in STEM education: Polynomials, Exponential, Hyperbolic and Trigonometric, as well as their inverses. The properties of polynomials and their derivatives and integrals can be easily established from Calculus. Exponential function is defined here in terms of the sum of infinite series. Again, the derivative and integral are obtained in a straight forward manner. Hyperbolic functions are combinations of exponential functions with real exponents, while trigonometric functions are combinations of exponential functions with imaginary exponents. In this regard, Euler's Formula is very useful

$$e^{i\theta} = \cos(\theta) + i\sin(\theta).$$

It turns out there are other ways to define and calculate elementary functions using their differential equations. First, from Calculus, the exponential function, $u(t) = e^t$, has the property $du/dt = u$. Together with the condition, $u(0) = 1$ we can calculate $u(t)$ at any point t. Namely, $u(t) = e^t$ is the solution to a differential equation. In this sense, the elementary function is defined by its differential equation up to a constant.

Similarly, the hyperbolic functions $\sinh(t)$ and $\cosh(t)$ and the trigonometric functions $\sin(t)$ and $\cos(t)$ can be calculated from the differential equation

$$\frac{d^2 u}{dt^2} + \alpha u = 0$$

where $\alpha = \mp 1$, and the initial conditions $u(0)$, $\frac{du}{dt}(0)$. Notice we have two constants of integration because we have to integrate the equation twice.

We also consider the differential equation

$$m\frac{d^2 u}{dt^2} + c\frac{du}{dt} + ku = 0,$$

which represents a mass-spring-damping system. An analogous system represents electrical circuits and is given by

$$L\frac{d^2 I}{dt^2} + R\frac{dI}{dt} + \frac{1}{C}I = 0,$$

where L is inductance, R is resistance, C is capacitance, and I is the current. This equation is heavily used in analog computers. The solution of both these equations is also an exponential function where, in general, the exponent is a complex number. For example, to find that solution analytically we assume the solution in the form

$$u(t) = u_0 e^{\lambda t}.$$

Substituting this form into the equation yields the algebraic (characteristic) equation for λ

$$m\lambda^2 + c\lambda + k = 0.$$

This quadratic equation has two roots, and therefore there are two possibilities. The solution $u(t)$ is a weighted combination of these two possibilities, and we need two conditions to determine the two weights involved. (There is also a special treatment for the case of real repeated roots.) The quadratic equation, has the solutions

$$\lambda_{1,2} = \frac{-c \pm \sqrt{c^2 - 4mk}}{2m}.$$

The solution will decay only if the real part of the λ is negative. To guarantee the stability of the solution, which implies that if the system is disturbed by small perturbations, the perturbations will eventually die out, the spring constant k must be positive to represent a restoring force. Similarly, the damping coefficient c must be positive, to represent loss of energy.

22.3   Numerical Methods

We started with the numerical methods for approximations of integrals and derivatives of given functions. The process consists of three steps: discretization of the domain, discretization of the integral (or the derivative), and calculation of the approximations. Discretization of the domain (or the grid generation) is simply replacing the infinite points of the domain of interest with a finite number of points, or nodes. Then the graph of the function is replaced by a part of a polygon. This step requires the values of the function at each of the nodes, and then connecting these values by straight lines. To approximate the derivative of the function, in any element between two nodes, we use the slope of the chord in this element. To find the integral of the function between any two node, the area under the curve is approximated by the area under a straight line. The more points that are used, the more accurate the approximation will be, assuming the function is smooth. In the above, the area under the polygon is simply evaluated by summing the areas of the trapezoids (Trapezoidal Rule). Other rules are discussed in the text, including rectangular rules (Riemann Sum).

Notice that a definite integral is a global quantity, while the derivative of the function is a local quantity. Also, if the derivative is required at the node, we can use the average of the slopes in the right and left element associated with the node. Using the above approximations for the elementary functions, we can calculate numerical approximations for their integrals and derivatives.

Now we come to the most important task. We do not have the function to approximate the derivatives and integrals, but instead we have the differential equation, or the corresponding integral equation. For example, we have

$$\frac{df}{dt} = g(f, t)$$

or, the equivalent form

$$f(t) - f(t_0) = \int_{t_0}^{t} g(f, \tau)d\tau.$$

The first is a differential equation involving a function and its derivatives, while the second is an integral equation involving the function and its integral. To solve the first form numerically we need numerical approximation of derivatives, while the numerical solution of the second form needs numerical approximations of integrals. Both ways can give the same numerical solution with proper choices for the approximations involved.

Next we introduced several choices for these approximations, and applied them in four modules. The first module is simply the first order scalar differential equations with a constant of integration defined by the function given at a starting point (initial value problem). The extension to a system of first order equations is also considered, and numerically treated using the same numerical approximation for the derivatives. The second module is a second order differential equation, with two initial conditions defined at the starting point. This module is a special case of two first order differential equations. The third module is a second order differential equation with the conditions given at the boundary of the domain (boundary value problem). The fourth module is a special case of the boundary value problem, and we use the buckling of a column under compressive load as an example. In this module, there is a trivial solution where the column is not buckled, and we are looking for a non-trivial solution. However, besides the shape of the buckled column (the eigenfunction), there is a critical value for the compressive load which is unknown (eigen or characteristic value). In all these four modules, we use the same strategy consisting of the three steps: the grid, the scheme, and the solver. Discretizing the domain, discretizing the equation and solving the discrete equations to approximate the solution.

Notice that for initial value problems we have two issues, first the accuracy of the numerical approximations, and we use Taylor Series expansion to study the accuracy of the schemes. Second, there is also an issue of numerical stability, which could be more restrictive than accuracy requirements. We give examples of several schemes for numerical solutions that have different accuracy, for both first order and second order differential equations.

We studied the discrete equations given in the recursive form

$$au_{n+1} + bu_n + cu_{n-1} = 0,$$

where n refers to the nth time step. Assuming $u_n = u_0 \Lambda^n$, and substituting in the above equation, we obtain a quadratic equation for Λ

$$a\Lambda^2 + b\Lambda + c = 0.$$

To guarantee numerical stability, where the absolute value of the error will not grow, we must satisfy the condition that $|\Lambda| < 1$.

Contrary to the initial value problems where we use recursive relations to obtain the solution by marching in time, for boundary value problems we need to solve the discrete (algebraic) equations simultaneously coupled together in space with techniques from linear algebra (for example Gaussian Elimination).

In the appendix, we have included a pseudo-code for Gaussian Elimination of tridiagonal matrix equations (Thomas Algorithm), which is heavily used for the solutions of second order boundary value problems. In these problems, every point is affected by its neighbors from the left and from the right, hence we have the coupled tridiagonal equations to solve. The code is very simple and consists of only two loops and four lines, yet it is very useful.

22.4 Numerical Solutions of Differential Equations

The strategies introduced in the four modules are used in the rest of the book. For the numerical solution of linear differential equations with constant coefficients representing mass-spring-damping system, we studied free and forced vibration, including well known examples of pure resonance, beating phenomenon, gyroscopic effects, etc. For linear differential equations with variable coefficients, we studied special functions, including Airy Function, Bessel Function, Legendre Polynomials and Mathieu Equations. For nonlinear differential equations we studied bifurcations: saddle node, transcritical, pitchfork, and Hopf (limit cycles).

Chaotic behavior is shown for the Jerk and for the Lorenz equations, where the solutions are aperiodic, unpredictable, and sensitive to initial conditions (SIC). We also studied nonlinear springs and nonlinear damping, including Duffing, Van der Pol, and Rayleigh oscillators. Moreover, we studied linear and non-linear boundary value problems, including second order equations with small parameters (singular perturbation) using Gaussian Elimination.

All these examples are presented to demonstrate the power and versatility of the simple numerical methods we used, in particular, for nonlinear problems where analytical solutions are not available in general.

22.5   Applications in Science and Engineering

First we have the dynamics of rockets, satellites and airplanes. This section is followed by structural mechanics, including tension in cables, bending of beams, torsion of shafts and buckling of columns. For fluid mechanics we discussed viscous incompressible flows in a channel, boundary layer over a flat plate, compressible flow in a convergent divergent nozzle and shock viscous layer. For heat transfer, we have examples for Newton's Law of Cooling for convection problems, Fourier law for heat conduction, and Stefan-Boltzmann law for heat radiation, and some examples for their combined effects. For chemical reaction we solved the differential equation representing one-step reactions (scalar equation), as well examples for several species (system of equations). Chemical oscillations and chemical chaos examples (Rossler) are also studied. Finally, we studied combustion problems with examples of thermal explosion theory and ignition based on Newton's cooling law and Fourier's conduction law combined with Arrhenius kinetics for heat production. Solid propellant burning is also considered in this section, where the accumulation of mass in the combustion chamber (rather than heat) is problematic.

Last, but not least, the book includes 50 brief biographies of eminent mathematicians, scientists and engineers whose works are relevant to the materials covered in this book. This biography section deals with the fascinating history of math and science from the ancient world to modern times.

We hope we will meet again to study Calculus next for functions with several variables, partial derivatives, partial differential equations, and their applications.

23. Appendices

23.1   Basics of Programming

There are many good references on programming. In principle just about any programming language could be used to work through this book. The basics of programming are summarized here.

1. Write a program, compile it (if necessary), and execute it.
2. Variable declaration: Vectors, Matrices, Indexing conventions
3. Basic Arithmetic operations
4. Vectorization and vector operations
5. Looping (for, while commands)
6. Conditional statements (if, else)
7. Built in functions (sin, cos, tan, exp)
8. Built in solvers and subroutines (Thomas algorithm)
9. Output, Plotting and Labeling
10. Debugging and validating results

For organization purposes, the use of flow charts and modular programming are highly recommended.

23.2   Thomas Algorithm for Tridiagonal Matrix

Here are the pseudo program for:

$$Ax = d,$$

where A is tridiagonal matrix with diagonal elements $b(n)$ and sub diagonal $a(n-1)$ and super diagonal $c(n-1)$. Here x is a vector of n components $x(n)$, and the right-hand side has components $d(n)$.

Algorithm:
Input: values of the vectors $a, b, c, d,$ of size n. Allocate storage for vectors bb, cc, dd, x.

Let $bb(1) = b(1), cc(1) = c(1), dd(1) = d(1)$.
Also $a(1) = 0$ and $c(n) = 0$

Do for $i = 2$ to n
    $bb(i) = b(i) - a(i) \cdot cc(i-1)/bb(i-1)$
    $cc(i) = c(i)$
    $dd(i) = d(i) - a(i) \cdot dd(i-1)/bb(i-1)$
End of loop

$x(n) = dd(n)/bb(n)$

Do for $j = 1$ to $n - 1$
    $i = n - j$
    $x(i) = [dd(i) - cc(i) \cdot x(i+1)]/bb(i)$
End of loop.

Print $x(i)$ from $i = 1$ to n.

To test the program use Excel or MATLAB and different values for $n = 20, 40, 80 \ldots$, for the tridiagonal matrix : $a(i) = 1$, $b(i) = -2$ and $c(i) = 1$, and $d(i) = 0$, except $d(1) = -1$ and $d(n) = -1$. The exact answer is $x(i) = 1$ for $i = 1$ to n.

24. General References

24.1 Math

1. Boyce, W.E., DiPrima, R.C. *Elementary Differential Equations and Boundary Value Problems.* John Wiley & Sons (2012)
2. Chapra, S.C. *Applied Numerical Methods with MATLAB for Engineers and Scientists.* McGraw-Hil, New York (2008)
3. Gelfand, I.M., Shen, A. *Algebra.* Birkhauser (2004)
4. Harvey, M. *Geometry Illuminated.* American Mathematical Society (2015)
5. Kolman, B. *Introductory Linear Algebra: An Applied First Course.* Prentice Hall (2004)
6. Kreyszig, E. *Advanced Engineering Mathematics.* John Wiley & Sons (2011)
7. Rex, A., Jackson, M. *Integrated Physics and Calculus, Volumes 1,2.* Addison-Wesley (1999)

8. Strang, G. *Introduction to Applied Mathematics*. Wellesley-Cambridge Press (1986)
9. Strogatz, S. *Nonlinear Dynamics and Chaos*. Westview Press (2014)
10. Thomas Jr., G.B., Weir, M.D., Hass, J.R. *Thomas Calculus*. Pearson (2014)

24.2 Science and Engineering

1. Brown, T.E. *et al.*, *Chemistry: The Central Science*. Pearson (2014)
2. Crandall, S.H. *et al.*, An Introduction to Mechanics of Solids. McGraw Hill Education (2012)
3. Gianocoli, D.C. *Physics for Scientists and Engineers with Modern Physics*. Pearson (2008)
4. Inman, D.J. *Engineering Vibration*. Pearson (2014)
5. Meriam, J.L, Kraige, L.G. *Engineering Mechanics: Statics*. Wiley (2014)
6. Meriam, J.L, Kraige, L.G. *Engineering Mechanics: Dynamics*. Wiley (2015)
7. Warnatz, J., Maas, U., Dibble, R.W. *Combustion: Physical and Chemical Fundamentals, Modeling and Simulation, Experiments, Pollutant Formation*. Springer (1999)
8. Incropera, F.P., DeWitt, D.P., Bergman, T.L., Lavine, A.S. *Fundamentals of Heat and Mass Transfer*. John Wiley & Sons (2006)
9. Moran, M.J., Shapiro, H.N. *Fundamentals of Engineering Thermodynamics*. John Wiley & Sons (2006)
10. White, F. *Fluid Mechanics*. McGraw-Hill (2008)

Index

Abel–Ruffini theorem, 22
ablation, 137
acceleration, 35, 110, 118
aerodynamics, 112, 116
airy functions, 71
Archimedes, 25
Arrhenius Law, 143, 145

beating, 57
bending, 38, 43, 122
Bernoulli equation, 82
Bernoulli's law, 129
Bessel functions, 71
bifurcations: Hopf, 87
bifurcations: Pitchfork, 86
bifurcations: Saddle Node, 84
bifurcations: Transcritical, 85
boundary conditions, 43
boundary layer, 77
boundary value problems, 68, 102
buckling, 45, 124

calculus, 25
channel flow, 43
chaos, 88, 89
characteristic equation, 54
characteristic value, 54
chemical reactions, 40, 138–141
combustion, 143, 145, 146
conduction: Fourier Law, 43, 135, 145
conservation
    conservation of energy, 116
    conservation of mass, 107, 128
    conservation of momentum, 129
    conservation of number of
        atoms, 196
convergent divergent nozzle, 129
Cramer's rule 12, 14
curvature, 37, 38, 122, 124

damping force, 42, 54, 55, 59, 63, 96,
    116

derivatives, 25, 28
difference schemes
    backward difference, 39
    central difference, 39
    forward difference, 39
    predictor-corrector, 39, 48
differential equations
    first order, 39
    second order BVP, 43
    second order IVP, 42
    summary, 29, 34
    system of first order, 41
discrete equations, 35, 127
discretization of equations, 35
drag, 112, 116
Duffing oscillator, 95
dynamic stability, 116
dynamical systems, chemical
    reactions, 41
dynamics, 107, 109, 110, 112, 113, 115

eigenvalue, 54
eigenvalue problems (characteristic
    value problems), 45
electrical circuits, 42, 58
electrical circuits, 42, 58
elementary functions, 12
entropy, 129
equilibrium
    neutrally stable, 87, 140
    stable and unstable equilibrium,
        146
    stable equilibrium, 119, 138, 139,
        143
Euler formula 12
Euler–Cauchy equation, 73
exponential function, 12, 31

fictitious point, 44
finite time blow-up, 78
fluid mechanics, 126, 128, 131
fractals, 20

fundamental theorem of algebra, 11
fundamental theorem of geometry, 11
fundamental theorems of calculus,
    2, 3, 12

gas constant, R, 129
Gaussian elimination, 14, 22
global positioning system, 24
grid generation, 41
gyroscopic effect, 63

heat radiation, 40
heat transfer, 132–135, 137
hyperbolic functions, 12, 31

ignition, 145
initial conditions, 42
integrals, 25
isentropic relation, 129

Jerk equation, 88

Kepler's equation, 20
kinetic energy, 116
Kirchhoff's laws, 58

landing gears, 65
law of mass action, 138, 195
Legendre polynomials, 77
lift, 116
linear algebra 12, 14
linearization, 20
logistic growth, 82
Lorenz equations, 89

mach number, 130
mass spring system, 42, 54–58
Mathieu equation, 72
moment, 38, 122, 124
momentum, 107, 129
multi-stage rocket, 109

natural frequency, 56
Newton's cooling law, 40, 133,
    134, 143
Newton's method, 14, 22–24

Newton's second law, 35
Newton's viscosity law, 126
nonlinear equations, 78
numerical methods, 35
numerical stability, 47

orbital mechanics, 42

parachutist, 40, 110
pendulums, 42, 92, 116
perfect gas law, 129
phugoid motion, 115, 116
polynomials, 22, 29
potential energy, 116
projectiles, 42, 110
propellant, 146

radiation, 133, 134
ratio of specific heat, γ, 129
Rayleigh equation, 100
Rayleigh oscillator equation, 96
rectangular rules, 25
relativistic space flight, 101
resonance, 56
restoring force, 55, 118, 120
Reynold's number, 126
rockets, 40, 107, 109
Rossler equations, 141

shock waves, 131
simple harmonic motion, 52, 115, 116
singular perturbation, 100
special functions, 34, 71, 77
speed, 111, 112, 116, 130
speed of sound, 130
stability of motion, 54, 115, 116
stability of orbits, 115
static stability, 119
structural mechanics, 120, 122–124

tangent, 37, 118
Taylor series, 13
tension, 43
thermal explosions, 143
thermal ignition, 143

torsion, 43, 123
trapezoidal rule, 25, 48
trigonometric functions, 31
trivial solution, 45, 82, 124
Tsiolkovsky equation, 107, 109
two-body problem, 113

Van der Pol oscillator, 96
velocity, 96, 101, 107, 109, 111, 112,
    116, 118, 126, 128
vibrations, 107

wind tunnel, 119

Printed in the United States
by Bookmasters

Printed in the United States
By Bookmasters